# Vancouver

*A Pictorial Celebration*

by Constance Brissenden

*Photography by Elan Penn*

Sterling Publishing Co., New York
A Sterling Book

Penn Publishing gratefully acknowledges the following institutions and individuals for allowing photographs from their collections to be reproduced in this book:

Craigdarroch Castle  59
Fairmont Empress Hotel  63
Gunter Marx Photography/CORBIS  121
The Butchard Gardens Ltd.  16, 64
The Royal British Columbia Museum  66-67
Tourism Whistler
Bonny Makarewicz  145
Greg  Eydmundson  147, 155
Greg  Griffith  146, 154
Vancouver Public Library 6-15, 18-25

Design by Michel Opatowski
Edited by J. E. Sigler
Layout by Gala Pre Press Ltd.

**Library of Congress Cataloging-in-Publication Data**

Brissenden, Connie
 Vancouver : a pictorial celebration, including Vancouver Island,
Victoria & Whistler / Constance Brissenden ; photography by Elan Penn.
 p. cm.
Includes index
 ISBN-13: 978-1-4027-2386-5
 ISBN-10: 1-4027-2386-5
 1. Vancouver (B.C.)—History. 2. Vancouver (B.C.)—Pictorial works.
3. Vancouver (B.C.)—Buildings, structures, etc. 4. Historic buildings—British
Columbia—Vancouver. 5. Vancouver Islands (B.C.)—History. 6. Vancouver
Island (B.C.)—Pictorial works. I. Penn, Elan. II. Title.

F1089.5.V22B75 2006
971.1'33—dc22                                           2005056321

2  4  6  8  10  9  7  5  3  1

Published by Sterling Publishing Co., Inc.
387 Park Avenue South, New York, NY 10016
© 2006 by Penn Publishing Ltd.
Distributed in Canada by Sterling Publishing
c/o Canadian Manda Group, 165 Dufferin Street
Toronto, Ontario, Canada M6K 3H6
Distributed in the United Kingdom by GMC Distribution Services
Castle Place, 166 High Street, Lewes, East Sussex, England BN7 1XU
Distributed in Australia by Capricorn Link (Australia) Pty. Ltd.
P.O. Box 704, Windsor, NSW 2756, Australia

Sterling ISBN-13: 1-987-1-4027-2386-5
ISBN-10: 1-4027-2386-5

For information about custom editions, special sales, premium and
corporate purchases, please contact Sterling Special Sales
Department at 800-805-5489 or specialsales@sterlingpub.com.

*Opposite: Flag Pole Plaza, University of British Columbia.*

# Contents

# Vancouver including Vancouver Island, Victoria, and Whistler "By Sea, Land and Air We Prosper"

Vancouver, Canada's "Gateway to the Pacific," is a young city. In 1865, few imagined that this small logging mill on the forested shore of Burrard Inlet would one day be the site of Canada's third-largest city. The first European explorers to this area discovered a 16,777-mile coastline edged by dense forests of ancient trees. Animals of every description were bountiful everywhere they looked: in the ocean and rivers, on land, and even in the air. Captain George Vancouver, who meticulously mapped the coastline in 1792, proclaimed, "I cannot possibly believe that any uncultivated country had ever been discovered exhibiting so rich a picture."

Long before colonization, for 10,000 years or more, aboriginal people inhabited the West Coast. Where Whistler Resort has blossomed 75 miles north of Vancouver, Interior Salish used to cross the Coast Mountain range along a trading route between the temperate rainforests of the Pacific and the arid interior regions. Many tribes still inhabit their traditional lands, among them the Coast Salish on the south coast, the Nuu-Chah-Nulth of Vancouver Island, and the Haida of the Queen Charlotte Islands. They, of course, have always known what Captain Vancouver did not discover until the eighteenth century: living on this land is virtually a guarantee of prosperity.

British Columbia's physical features have played a determining role in its history. The old-growth forests of the North Shore and the bountiful salmon runs of the Fraser River paved the way for enterprise and exploitation. The Pacific Ocean connects the city to international trading partners, particularly along the Pacific

*Car rally in Stanley Park, circa 1904. Photographed by Philip Timms.*

2056

*Horseshoe Bay, circa 1912. Photographed by Leonard Frank.*

Rim. The once almost insurmountable Coast Mountain range, now home to Whistler, appears to have been destined for isolated, relaxed resort living. And with the warmest year-round climate in Canada, outdoor sports and recreation were bound to make their way to British Columbia sooner or later. As the province's motto declares: "By Sea, Land and Air We Prosper." Actually, without them, we would not be here at all.

## From Tribal Territory to Queen's Capital: Exploration & Discovery

The west coast of North America was a busy place in the late 1700s. Spanish ships sailed north from Mexico, Russians ventured south from Siberia, and the great explorer Captain James Cook led the way for Britain. On March 31, 1778, Cook's ships found safe anchorage at Nootka Sound, midway up the west coast of Vancouver Island. Maquinna, the chief of the Mowachaht people of Nootka Sound, welcomed Cook and his men. Other tribes extended the same courtesy to subsequent Europeans, including the Kwakwaka'wakw people, who met George Vancouver while he was circumnavigating Vancouver Island in 1792. Both men to make initial British contact with local aboriginal peoples are honored by statues in the province's capital, Victoria: Captain Cook looks out over the Inner Harbour, while Captain Vancouver graces the top of the British Columbia (B.C.) Parliament Buildings.

Like every Native tribe in Canada, these two island peoples were destined to come under European domination. The Nimpkish Burial Grounds in Alert Bay are mute testimony to Kwakwaka'wakw history. But they are also a powerful symbol of the general history of all indigenous peoples in Canada. Traditionally, the Kwakwaka'wakw's deceased were folded into carved boxes or canoes and left above ground, often in trees. With colonization, traditional practices were discouraged, and assimilation was even violently enforced. At Nimpkish Burial Grounds, one can see how the traditional burial practices of the Kwakwaka'wakw were replaced by Christian underground burial. Today, thankfully, the struggles of First Nations peoples for respect and recognition have succeeded in fostering increased tolerance and appreciation for diversity, which in turn has led to a Native cultural and artistic revival across the province. The Mowachaht/Muchalaht people are still a strong presence in the Clayoquot Sound area, and they continue to visit their traditional summer home on Vargas Island near the town of Tofino.

British Columbia's resource wealth was Britain's prize for colonization, and it was taken advantage of very quickly. On Vancouver Island, a vibrant trade in sea otter pelts, then industries such as logging, mining, salmon fishing, and whaling were established. Many island towns like Duncan date back to the 1880s, when giant Douglas firs were first being logged. Logging and fishing are still two of the most important industries on the island, but over time, the rules of the game have changed. Just as increased awareness of human rights and appreciation of indigenous cultures has enabled Canada's original inhabitants to flourish again, environmental awareness has curbed the worst excesses of the exploitation of natural resources. In the 1990s, after a long campaign demanding protection of its old-growth trees, Clayoquot Sound was designated a UNESCO Biosphere Reserve. Throughout the province, parks, people, the B.C. government, and forestry companies now work together to sort out their often conflicting goals for the longterm preservation of the magnificent West Coast forests.

The lucrativeness of the fur trade and subsequent industries on Vancouver Island necessitated protection. That protection came in 1843, when Fort Victoria, the predecessor of the British Columbian capital, was established at what is now Bastion Square. The most influential European residents at this time were the employees of the fur-trading Hudson's Bay Company, all proper married men with homes and families. But they were not the majority: most of the island's inhabitants were sailors, ne'er-do-wells, fishermen, prostitutes, and saloon keepers. Soon there would come a wholly new species of settler, too: the gold prospector.

In response to the Fraser River Gold Rush and the influx of immigrants, Fort Victoria's original purpose was considerably upgraded in importance. In 1856, the now-booming town that had grown up around the fort was designated the colonial capital of Vancouver Island. In addition to many other buildings thrown up to accommodate all the newcomers, the Fisgard Lighthouse near Victoria was built to safeguard increasing marine traffic. Chinatown was born in these days as well, tossed together by the wave of Asian immigrants looking for a better life in "Gold Mountain."

As quickly as it had come, though, the Gold Rush also went. Some of the prospectors liked the area so much that they stayed, but many of those who had come returned to whence they came. Many more couldn't afford to go

*Three logs on a flat car at Comox Logging Company on Vancouver Island, circa 1919. Photographed by Leonard Frank.*

anywhere, not having made it quite as big in the gold fields as they'd hoped. The Chinese were one such group: by the 1880s, some 20,000 were building the Canadian Pacific Railway (CPR) line into Vancouver. Short-lived as the Gold Rush was, its effects were very long indeed: in 1866, Victoria was named the capital of the colony of British Columbia, and in 1871, after joining the Dominion of Canada, it became the provincial capital.

### Building the British Empire: The Victorian Era in Victoria's City

During the Victorian era, from Queen Victoria's ascension to the throne in 1836 to her death in 1901, the little city named for her did its best to maintain the traditions of the mother country. In fact, Victoria's populace has been described as "more British than the British." Progress came house by house, beginning with pretty clapboard edifices such as the James Bay birthplace of artist Emily Carr. In Victoria's early years, James Bay was the desirable place to live; in death, the elegant Ross Bay Cemetery was the only place for Victoria's good citizens to rest. The city's Chinese dead were interred farther along Dallas Road in the Chinese Cemetery at Harling Point.

Wealth and fame came to some in Victoria, but this was a rugged era, so they usually did not come smoothly. The Victorian era was obsessed with scandals, and the city had its share. Craigdarroch Castle, the "Rocky Oak Place" in Gaelic, was the scene of financial battles between Joan Dunsmuir, widow of millionaire industrialist Robert Dunsmuir, and her eldest son, James. Then there was architect Francis Mawson

Rattenbury, who left his wife for a younger woman, Emma Pakenham, while he was in his mid-sixties. Emma's lover, an 18-year-old chauffeur, ultimately murdered Rattenbury in England in 1935. Both the British Columbia (B.C.) Parliament Buildings and the Fairmont Empress Hotel were designed by Rattenbury and remain a striking testimony to his genius—as well as reminders of his appalling demise.

Even today, Victoria remains true to its British and Victorian roots. Of all of British Columbia's cities, it has preserved the most century-old buildings. Since 1886, when a group of businessmen founded the Provincial Museum, today's famed Royal British Columbia Museum, residents themselves have staunchly protected their European history. But they also learned to appreciate that of their Native neighbors: from its earliest days, the Royal British Columbia Museum included examples of impressive aboriginal art, such as dance masks and house poles. Several poles now stand in the museum's Thunderbird Park. The Art Gallery of Greater Victoria, with its collection of Canadian and Asian works, preserves other important aspects of Victoria's heritage.

## Manufactured by the CPR: Early Vancouver

The area known as Greater Vancouver, with 1.2 million residents, is the third-largest city in Canada after Toronto and Montreal. The city began life in 1865 as Stamp's Mill, a small sawmill along the tree-lined shores of Burrard Inlet. In the fall of 1867, John Deighton, a Yorkshire man, arrived here and opened a saloon. Nicknamed "Gassy Jack" for his volubility, Deighton was so beloved that his customers—a rambunctious mix of mill workers, sailors, and whalers—unofficially named the town for him: Gastown.

In 1870, Gastown was officially renamed Granville. The town grew so quickly that it took just 16 years to be incorporated as a city, called Vancouver. The name was bequeathed upon it by the president of the Canadian Pacific Railway (CPR), William Cornelius Van Horne, who wanted an impressive name for the terminus of his new transcontinental railway. "Terminal City," one of Vancouver's early nicknames, persists to this day.

The CPR's influence was felt across the city. The West End was developed on railway-owned property overlooking English Bay, home of some of the city's finest beaches. Today, the West End is dominated by high rises interrupted here and there by a few classic turn-of-the-century homes. Another of the city's up-scale neighborhoods, the wealthy enclave of Shaughnessy, was also developed on property purchased from the CPR. Other powerful entities significantly influenced other areas of development. For example, Vancouverites thank the affluent Guiness brewing family of Ireland for the impressive Lions Gate Bridge, which opened up access to the even more impressive mountain estates of the North Shore's British Properties.

These bastions of privilege stood in stark contrast to swampy Chinatown and working-class Mount Pleasant. Both were tainted by the smoke and smells of the mills and CPR foundries of Yaletown on the north shore of False Creek and by the industrial area now known as Granville Island on the south shore. Thankfully, conditions have improved considerably in all these areas: Vancouver's Chinatown is now the third-largest in North America and attracts swarms of locals and visitors to shop in its streets. Mount Pleasant is now a historic area bustling with trendy boutiques and eateries. And Yaletown and Granville Island have been redeveloped into livable urban communities with easy access to downtown.

The same year that the city of Vancouver was incorporated, the Great Fire burned it all down. City leaders were not discouraged, however: the very next day, they began building anew, this time of stone and brick. A real city, as opposed to the pre-fire shantytown, began to take shape. At that time, the city center was still on the waterfront in Gastown, so the majority of the reconstruction effort benefited that area. But, in 1887, when the CPR brought the first railway line into Vancouver, the city granted the company 6,000 acres of land that were mostly *not* on the waterfront. The timing worked out quite well for the CPR, which used the destruction and rebirth of the city as an opportunity to increase the value of its land holdings: by beginning several attention-grabbing construction and

*Parks Board Band in front of the Stanley Park Pavilion, August 2, 1925. Photographed by Leonard Frank.*

development projects on their land, they shifted settlement from the waterfront southward, to where downtown Vancouver is today.

Local political leaders also took advantage of the destruction, but not to line their pockets. They set aside 1,000 acres of land for the creation of Stanley Park, now the city's most famous landmark. The Vancouver Aquarium Marine Science Centre, an internationally renowned marine research and rescue facility, is a prominent resident in the park today. Vancouver's two other famous green spaces also began life in less than dignified capacities, but both of these owe their current glory to generous lumber magnates: Queen Elizabeth Park, once a rock quarry, received the prestigious Bloedel

*"The Sunken Garden at Butchart Gardens, 1926."*

Floral Conservatory thanks to a $1.25 million donation from Prentice Bloedel; the VanDusen Botanical Garden was a golf course until Whitford Julian VanDusen gave $1 million to help turn it into a garden.

Vancouverites love and cherish their great green outdoors, but history and art are British Columbia obsessions. Nowhere are the province's origins better represented than at the University of British Columbia's Museum of Anthropology, with its 6,000 First Nations objects and programs that encourage First Nations artists to continue their traditional work. More local history is featured in the Vancouver Museum at Vanier Park, also the site of the H. R. MacMillan Space Centre and the H. R. MacMillan Planetarium. Both early and modern British Columbia artists are honored in collections at the Vancouver Art Gallery, housed in the former 1912 Provincial Court House designed by the ubiquitous Francis Mawson Rattenbury and rebuilt by the equally admired architect Arthur Erickson in 1983.

**Twentieth-Century Legacies: Downtown Vancouver & Beyond**

Downtown Vancouver is an agreeable mix of historic and modern buildings that cater to everyone from royalty and businessmen to tourists and students. Virtually all of today's downtown was part of the city's 6,000-acre land grant to the CPR, so the company was naturally the dominant force in the area's development. From the 1880s until 1939, the company opened three downtown hotels—each one more luxurious than the last—to house the crowds of affluent guests arriving at its three train stations—each one grander than the one before it. What remains today are Waterfront Station and the Fairmont Hotel Vancouver, whose guest list reads like a celebrity's little black book.

Vancouver's notable modern buildings are an eclectic group. The 1977 Harbour Centre, with its 581-foot tower with lookout, boasts of being the city's tallest structure. Expo 86, Vancouver's hugely successful 1986 world exposition, bequeathed many unique buildings to the public: the impressive B.C. Place Stadium, the largest air-supported stadium in North America; Canada Place, with its five sails modeled on the Sydney Opera House jutting out into Vancouver Harbour; and on the shores of False Creek, the geodesic-domed Expo Centre, now home to Science World.

Unlike many North American cities, Vancouver's interesting sites do not stop at the borders of downtown. In fact, both of the city's important universities are located outside the city center. Students at the University of British Columbia (UBC), the first university in the province, actually fought hard to obtain their scenic Point Grey campus in 1925. UBC is now a city in itself, with housing and classrooms for thousands, as well as plenty of shopping and dining. Burnaby Mountain is home to the isolated campus of Simon Fraser University, nicknamed "Radical U" when it opened in the 1960s, but now one of Canada's leading institutions of higher education.

It isn't necessary to go all the way to Whistler or Vancouver Island to have a little outdoor fun, either. The area of Vancouver known as the North Shore, located across Burrard Inlet from Vancouver, has 15 mountain peaks with spectacular vistas. Grouse Mountain was the first mountain in the area developed for outdoor activities, and its views are still the best known. It is now a year-round attraction, combining skiing in winter with hiking in summer. The Capilano Suspension Bridge is also located in North Vancouver. The swaying suspension bridge—the longest and highest in the world—and the surrounding park's totem poles and fascinating treetop walks have been named British Columbia's best and most innovative outdoor attractions. Picturesque Horseshoe Bay on the North Shore in West Vancouver is also worth a visit when getting out of town.

*Lions Gate Bridge under construction, with the* Empress of Japan II *passing underneath, 1938. Photographed by Leonard Frank.*

*Previous page: Opening of the Burrard Street Bridge, July 1932. Photographed by Leonard Frank.*

**The Great Outdoors: Whistler**

Beyond Horseshoe Bay, the Sea to Sky Highway (Highway 99) winds along Howe Sound into the Coast Mountains. The road rises from sea level to 2,214 feet in Whistler, 75 miles from Vancouver. Few routes are as beautiful as this one, and travelers should be sure to make frequent stops. At Shannon Falls Provincial Park, cascading glacial waters fall more than 1,105 feet over a rocky precipice. The Stawamus Chief, a granite monolith south of the town of Squamish, is a favorite of hikers and rock climbers. To the local Coast Salish people, "the Chief" looks like a man sleeping on his side.

Squamish is now home to more than 15,000 people. Just 43 miles north of Vancouver, the mountain town is located at the top of Howe Sound, a fjord-like body of water more than 25 miles long. The town's proximity to Whistler makes it a bedroom community for the resort, but the "Gateway to Recreation," as Squamish is called, offers plenty to do itself: hiking, rock climbing, windsurfing, mountain biking, and glacier skiing are just a few of the outdoor sports enjoyed here. A bit farther up the road to Whistler, the magnificent Mt. Tantalus, the highest peak in the Tantalus Mountain Range of the Coast Mountains, reveals its peak at 8,540 feet above sea level. Very experienced climbers take at least three days to reach the peak.

Whistler traces its roots as a resort paradise to the popular Alta Lake Rainbow Lodge, opened by Alex and Myrtle Philip in 1914. When the Pacific Great Eastern Railway pushed through to their area from Squamish, Rainbow Lodge became the most popular resort west of the Rocky Mountains. Simply said: it put Whistler on the map. The Philips' resort no longer stands, but Rainbow Park and the River of Golden Dreams commemorate their enormous contribution to the area.

Ten years after the Philips retired in 1948, public interest in the mountains swung from summer to winter activities. In 1959, the Tyrol Ski Club opened, and from that point on development moved swiftly. In 1966, Franz Wilhelmsen's Garibaldi Lift Company opened up Whistler Mountain to the masses. In 1975, Alta Lake's name was officially changed to Whistler, and the Resort Municipality of Whistler was incorporated—still the only resort in Canada with this special designation. In 1980, Blackcomb Mountain opened next to Whistler Mountain, doubling the area's ski capacity.

More than 12,000 people now live and work in Whistler year-round. The number of inhabitants swells to nearly 30,000 at peak times of the year. In all, two million people visit Whistler's "Mile High Mountains" annually. The little lake resort that started as a place for Vancouverites to fish now welcomes international visitors with a wide variety of year-round activities, not to mention four luxurious villages complete with shops and all manner of dining and entertainment. Without a doubt, Whistler's high-speed lifts to the high alpine are among the resort's most-appreciated assets. The Whistler Village Gondola takes a 20-minute ride to the top of Whistler Mountain, climbing 1,100 feet per minute to its destination 6,000 feet above. Altogether, the combined lifts of Whistler and Blackcomb Mountains can carry more than 59,000 skiers per hour—but the views from the lifts are not to be missed even by non-skiers!

Over the years, Whistler's outdoor recreational offerings have been developed and diversified. Several trails, including Valley Trail and the Lost Lake Loop, were developed for visitors by local residents themselves. Entrepreneurs keep an eye out for new recreational activities to add to Whistler's repertoire, and their latest addition, a series of first-class golf courses, has met with rave reviews. As tourism to the area has increased, park rangers have learned that they must meticulously preserve their natural heritages so that they will not be adversely affected by the nearby traffic. Their special efforts have resulted in some of the best-maintained and most exciting forests, parks, and natural habitats on the continent.

In 2010, Whistler joins Vancouver to invite the world to the Olympic and Paralympic Winter Games. The decision ensures that the entire area will continue to develop, adding to its already remarkable assets. In the meantime, the south coast of British Columbia continues to grow. Together, Vancouver, Victoria, and Whistler express the vibrancy of a young province still filled with hopes and dreams for the future.

But what makes this prosperous coast so unique is not its bright future alone. Vancouver's precious landmarks are proof that the province has struck a near-perfect balance between honoring its history and striving ahead. Vancouver Island's vibrant mix of cultures—Native, European, and Asian—testify to efforts to both nurture its roots and welcome newcomers. And Whistler's still-pristine natural beauty is evidence that locals take care to give back to the land as much as it gives to them. These outstanding achievements are the reason why Greater Vancouver is recognized today as one of the world's most livable cities. And they're the reason why millions of visitors stream toward the Pacific Coast of Canada. Mother Nature's refreshing seas, breathtaking land, and invigorating air are just the beginning: wait and see what British Columbians will do with them!

*Georgia Street in the snow, circa 1900.*
*Photographed by Philip Timms.*

*Previous page: Looking north from Hotel*
*Vancouver, 1940. Stanley Park and Coal*
*Harbour are visible at left. Burrard Inlet and the*
*Marine Building are visible at center, along with*
*several smaller buildings and houses.*
*Photographed by Philip Timms.*

From Tribal Territory to
Queen's Capital: Exploration
& Discovery

## Captain James Cook Statue

"I had ambition not only to go farther than any one had been before, but as far as it was possible for man to go." Captain James Cook achieved his ambition, making three voyages to the Pacific Ocean and beyond. The British explorer, surveyor, and mapmaker is officially recognized as the first European visitor to the West Coast of Canada. He also made the first British contact with the Mowachaht (now known as Mowachaht/Muchalaht) people.

When Cook's vessel *Resolution* appeared in Nootka Sound on March 30, 1778, Mowachaht chief Maquinna and his people were living in their summer homes there. Chief Maquinna sent his warriors to investigate. When they returned, it is recalled that they told Maquinna, "You know, they

have white skin. But we're pretty sure that those people on the floating thing must have been fish."

Cook was also unsure of his hosts. When they arrived in their giant cedar canoes, they shouted at him to "go around, go around" to the safer bay of Friendly Cove. Cook thought they were telling him where he had landed, which sounded to him like "nootka." Thus Nootka Sound was named. Cook claimed the territory for Britain and traded with the clever and enterprising Maquinna. After leaving Nootka Sound, he went on to Hawai'i, where angry islanders murdered him on February 14, 1779.

Today, a statue of the captain overlooks Victoria's Inner Harbour, and many other memorials to him are scattered about the island.

*Previous page: Alert Bay.*

# Duncan

When the first Europeans arrived in the Duncan area, they found an estimated 6,000 Quw'utsun' people living in 13 villages. The word *Quw'utsun'*, meaning "the place warmed by the sun," became "Cowichan" when interpreted by early European settlers. These settlers established the town of Duncan in the 1880s, when it was a whistle-stop for the railway at William Duncan's farm.

Some 3,500 Quw'utsun' people still live here today, and the town has recently been dubbed the "City of Totems" for its abundance of totem poles carved by local Coast Salish artists. Since 1985, this largest of the Cowichan district communities and centers for First Nations heritage has proudly displayed the poles as a symbol of the local Native cultural reclamation. On their way through the valley north of Victoria, visitors are welcomed by more than 22 poles along Highway 1, the Trans-Canada Highway; another 60 poles are displayed at downtown locations.

The aboriginal people who carve the poles are the inheritors of a culture that dates back more than 4,500 years. Every one of their totem poles tells a story: Some represent ancestral tales about mythical creatures such as Killer Whale, Thunderbird, and Wild Woman of the Woods. Others depict an individual's life, telling of memorable personal events such as marriages or deaths. Local Coast Salish Natives are also known world-wide for their warm, hand-knit Cowichan sweaters. Totem poles, sweaters, beadwork, and weaving are displayed at the Quw'utsun' Cultural and Conference Centre in Duncan. The center's motto is "Come, Share Our Pride." Gatherings are held at the center in the Comeakin House, a longhouse built entirely of western red cedar.

*Totem poles in Duncan.*

# Clayoquot Sound

Located some 185 miles northwest of Victoria, Clayoquot (pronounced clack-wot) Sound is the largest area of ancient, unlogged temperate rainforest left on Vancouver Island. Western hemlock, Sitka spruce, and western red cedar trees—some of them as old as 1,700 years—have grown to 295 feet tall and 15 feet across.

Clayoquot is the anglicized name of the local Tla-O-Qui-Aht tribe. Three main First Nation groups live in the area: the Hesquiaht in the north, the Ahousaht in the center, and the Tla-O-Qui-Aht in the south. Their traditional territories of sea and land boast a wealth of natural riches, including Pacific salmon, orca (commonly known as killer whales), gray whales, Roosevelt elk, black bears, and wolves. Migrating waterfowl, eagles, and shorebirds are joined by the elusive, endangered marbled murrelet, a small seabird that nests in the coastal old-growth forests of the Pacific Northwest.

These irreplaceable trees and animals inspired the most significant act of peaceful civil disobedience in Canada's history. In 1993, 850 people were arrested for protesting proposed logging of the ancient forest. Their efforts finally met with success when, on May 5, 2000, Clayoquot Sound was designated a UNESCO Biosphere Reserve, deserving of protection for its terrestrial and marine ecosystems. At the inauguration ceremony, Jean Chretien, then Canadian prime minister, spoke movingly of the sound as "a place of wonder, one whose beauty takes the breath away. It fills you with a sense of our sacred responsibility as stewards of this very special place. Small wonder that its preservation has prompted such passion here and around the world." Although ecological threats remain, national and international awareness have now joined the area's Native peoples to support the preservation of this pristine heritage.

# Tofino

Tofino, at the entrance to Clayoquot Sound on the west coast of Vancouver Island, is a pretty village with only 1,600 permanent residents. Typical of the area are the boat-lined wharves where fresh seafood is sold straight off the fishing boats. Logging and fishing are the main industries. The area is a magnet for tourists, outdoor adventurers, and, in winter, storm watchers. Old-growth forests abound, white-sand beaches glisten in the sun, eagles soar overhead, black bears and wolves wander about, and every spring nearly 20,000 gray whales pass by the shore as they migrate to Baja, California.

In 1792, Tofino was named by explorer Juan Francisco de la Bodega y Quadra after his teacher, the Spanish hydrographer Vicente Tofino de San Miguel, rear admiral of the Spanish Naval Academy in Cadiz. The wild and rugged coast soon developed a reputation as the "Graveyard of the Pacific" for the many shipwrecks that occurred there. In 1932, Tofino was incorporated, and in 1959 a gravel road from Port Alberni made Tofino accessible by land to the rest of Vancouver Island.

The Wickaninnish Interpretive Centre on Long Beach introduces visitors to local natural history. Guided beach tours reveal the mysteries of saltwater life, and the center's displays include a collection of cultural objects of the Nuu-Chah-Nulth, the aboriginal people who live in this wild, impressive region. Five Nuu-Chah-Nulth villages are located nearby, with a total of 1,500 residents.

Arts and crafts are major components of coastal life. Local Tsimshian artist Roy Vickers is an internationally renowned painter and print-maker. His works are sold in Tofino's Eagle Aerie Gallery, a hand-hewn longhouse. The House of Himwitsa exhibits the works of other local Native artists, including totem poles, sculptures, masks, paintings, basketry, and jewelry. Many non-Native artists are also active in Tofino, producing original paintings, pottery, sculptures, carvings, metal work, and glass.

## Vargas Island

Vargas Island on Clayoquot Sound is only three miles northwest of Tofino, but the similarities end there. Vargas has no roads and no vehicles, and practically no people. The island's vast, isolated beaches and quiet coves are accessible only by boat, kayak, or floatplane. "It's easy to get away from people here. You are stepping back in time," says long-time resident and tour operator Kim Crosby of Wildheart Adventures. The Ahousat Nation of the Nuu-Chah-Nulth people, most of whom live on nearby Flores Island, enjoy traditional summer visits to this site on the east shore of Vargas Island at Yarksis.

The area's natural treasures are protected by the Vargas Island Provincial Park, established in 1995. The park encompasses 14,301 acres of foreshore and uplands, covering the rugged western portion of Vargas Island, Blunden Island, and the tiny La Croix Group of islands. Most of the island is fairly flat, but there are bogs in the central upland. With eight feet of rainfall every year, the island is cloaked in lush stands of conifers that have earned it distinction as the largest lowland temperate rainforest on earth. Hemlock, cedar, Sitka spruce, and Douglas fir stand tall against the sky. The coastline is defined by white-sand beaches, sheltered bays and channels, intertidal lagoons, and mudflats. Rocky outcrops contrast with the vivid blue waters of the Pacific Ocean. Bald eagles appear in large numbers in Clayoquot Sound because many nest on Vargas Island.

Medallion Beach is close to Tofino and so makes for an easy day trip from that village. Ahous Bay, the island's largest beach, is home to a Vancouver Island sub-species of grey wolves that draws swarms of lupus buffs. Under the Park and Recreation Area Regulations and the Wildlife Amendment Act, it is an offense to feed wildlife, but some wolves do become acclimatized to human interaction. In 2000, two young wolves who were unafraid to approach humans were destroyed after a rare attack on a visitor who was camping on the beach at Ahous Bay.

Beyond the pristine beaches, the Pacific Ocean teems with wildlife. Dall's porpoises, sea lions, and seals play in the windswept surf. Gray whales migrate along the coast to summer feeding grounds in the Arctic Ocean and Bering Sea. Sport fishermen from around the world enjoy the challenges of freshwater and saltwater fishing in the waters of Tofino and Clayoquet Sound.

# Alert Bay

Alert Bay, situated on the temperate south shore of crescent-shaped Cormorant Island just off the northeast coast of North Vancouver Island, is the oldest European settlement in this area. The bay's culture is the result of a mix of influences, but the original Coast Salish inhabitants, the Kwakwaka'wakw, remain a dominant force in the community of 1,500 people. Their presence is felt in the totem poles and other carvings, paintings, and metal work that reflect their ancient heritage here.

The Coast Salish people who lived here in the eighteenth century met Captain George Vancouver in 1792 after he anchored his vessel *Discover* at the mouth of the Nimpkish River. Nearby Cormorant Island was uninhabited at the time; in 1846, it was finally named after the *Cormorant* coastal cruiser. Alert Bay, on the other hand, was consequential enough to have had a name already: the Kwakwaka'wakw called it *Ya'Lis*, "Spreading-Leg Beach." However, in 1858, European settlers named it after another vessel, the *Alert*, and that's the name that is universally used today. European settlement of the bay area began in earnest in the late nineteenth century. By 1870, two entrepreneurs, Wesley Spencer and Aulden Huson, had leased Cormorant Island from the government and built a facility there to salt and mildcure salmon. With its deep, sheltered harbor and strategic location, Alert Bay quickly became a regular port of call.

When, in 1884, the government of Canada outlawed the potlatch ceremony—wealth-sharing ceremonies that mark births, marriages, deaths, and the transfer of names—it was believed the aboriginal way of life would not survive. For a time, potlatches went underground: In 1921, 45 people in Alert Bay were arrested for holding a potlatch. Ceremonial clothing and objects, including coppers representing status and wealth, dance masks, dance rattles, and whistles, were confiscated from them and distributed among museum and private collections around the world.

Changing times have brought an awareness and new respect for Native cultures and traditions. The Kwakwaka'wakw have successfully reclaimed and are now staunchly proud of their traditional art, dances, songs, legends, ceremonies, and language. Additionally, intense international efforts have resulted in the Kwakwaka'wakw bringing home much of their stolen property. The U'mista Cultural Centre in Alert Bay has become an internationally known facility housing one of the finest collections of these irreplaceable heritage objects. The longhouse-style main building is typical of communal dwellings on the West Coast.

Today, visitors come to Alert Bay to explore Native culture, to enjoy the West Coast scenery, and to engage in outdoor activities such as saltwater fishing. It is equally well traveled as the gateway to scenic Knight and Kingcome Inlets and the Broughton Archipelago, which is known for recreational activities such as deep-sea diving, kayaking, whale watching, and nature hikes.

## Nimpkish Burial Grounds

Seventeen carved red-cedar totem poles stand in the century-old Nimpkish Burial Grounds in Alert Bay. Visitors are not allowed on the grounds, but good views of the poles can still be had from the road and the bay. Each pole is a visual statement and a powerful record of the 'Namgis (also known as Nimpkish) First Nations, the Native people of Alert Bay. Most were raised in memory of deceased family or community members, but some honor a special event. The crest art featured on the poles represents family clans with creatures such as eagles, frogs, ravens, killer whales, and grizzly bears. Mythical creatures such as Thunderbird, Dzunuk'wa the Wild Woman, and Sisiyutl, a double-headed serpent, also appear.

By tradition, 'Namgis were laid to rest in bent cedar boxes that were stored in trees. Underground burials in the community began with the arrival of Christian missionaries. In the 1880s, the Canadian government made an attempt to stamp out indigenous cultures, and many poles were taken from the burial grounds; some were sold to museums around the world. The last burials at the Nimpkish Burial Grounds were in the late 1970s.

In spite of their often tragic circumstances, Northwest Coast cultures have survived, and are now experiencing a dynamic renewal. Poles are still being carved and raised with great ceremony, with entire villages attending. However, the carved poles are not maintained or repainted: if they fall or are damaged, the elders of Alert Bay say they have served their purpose.

# Goldstream Provincial Park

British Columbia is proud of its provincial parks. Goldstream Provincial Park in Langford is only 12 miles from downtown Victoria, yet its 327 acres of heavily forested landscape retain the natural elements that make the West Coast unique. Douglas firs more than 600 years old share the forest with impressive western red cedars and a host of smaller trees, such as the broadleaf maple, beach cottonwood, western yew, red alder, and western hemlock. A second distinct vegetation grows along coarse, stony ridges, where lodgepole pines and arbutus trees dominate. The unique arbutus, with its papery, peeling, reddish-brown bark, is the only broadleafed evergreen tree in Canada.

Use of the Goldstream area by human beings began thousands of years ago, when it served as a fall fishing ground for Coast Salish people. In the late 1850s and into the 1860s, the Gold Rush brought eager men searching for their fortune.

Trails through Goldstream Park lead past abandoned gold mines set amidst giant old-growth trees. Today's visitors hike, camp, swim, picnic, and fish in the park.

Goldstream is distinguished by its annual salmon run from late October through December. Thousands of coho, chum, and chinook salmon make their way from the Pacific Ocean to the Finlayson Arm of the Saanish Peninsula, then struggle up the Goldstream River to the place of their birth. Once they have achieved this monumental task, they spawn and fertilize their eggs, then die. Hoards of black bears and bald eagles hover nearby to feast on the carcasses, while fiesty seagulls pick up the leftovers. During the winter season, crowds of visitors come to watch the bald eagles sit in the trees next to the river's estuary; as many as 275 of the majestic birds have been seen in one day.

*Glaucous-winged gull at salmon run.*

## Helmcken House

It is easier to overlook the Helmcken home than it was to overlook Dr. John Sebastian Helmcken, a doctor, statesman, Hudson's Bay Company employee, and founder of the British Columbia Medical Society. Tucked in the shadow of the Royal British Columbia Museum, the simple clapboard building blends into the landscape. But it is, in fact, quite outstanding as the oldest house in British Columbia that still stands on its original site.

The house is characteristic of life in the outpost of Victoria in the early 1850s. Recently married, Dr. Helmcken built the home with old-growth Douglas fir trees from the forest that surrounded it. The family moved into the original three rooms in 1852, and over the years the house grew along with the family.

In 1939, the Province of British Columbia bought Helmcken House as a historic site. Now open to the public, the many original furnishings and personal belongings on display tell of a hard-working doctor who enjoyed the comforts of a British-style residence in a far-off Colonial land. Guided tours point out some of the house's highlights: the doctor's medical collection; a reproduction sofa in the parlor, where ladies gathered after dinner; the family's piano, still in working order; and old books, trunks, and toys stored in the attic.

# Captain George Vancouver Statue

From atop the copper dome of the British Columbia (B.C.) Parliament Buildings, a statue of Captain George Vancouver, one of the greatest explorers who ever lived, gazes out to the ocean whence he came. The British captain, explorer, and mapmaker arrived off the coast of what is now the city of Vancouver in June 1792. It would be four years and 93,000 miles before he would return home, but he would achieve some great accomplishments in the meantime: he proved without a doubt that the fabled Northwest Passage did not exist and became the first European to circumnavigate Vancouver Island, thereby confirming that it was indeed an island. He named it "Quadra and Vancouver Island" to honor his friendship with another Spanish captain, Juan Francisco de la Bodega y Quadra, but common usage has shortened the name to "Vancouver Island." On his long journey, Vancouver charted every bay, inlet, and other coastal feature along the way and named more than 400 of them, but it was his own name that would eventually be foremost on the West Coast: Fort Vancouver, Vancouver Island, the City of Vancouver, West Vancouver, and North Vancouver are all named after him.

*The Maritime Museum of British Columbia on Bastion Square.*

## Bastion Square

In 1843, Hudson's Bay Company (HBC) agent James Douglas established Fort Victoria on Vancouver Island. The fort quickly became HBC's main Pacific fur trading post, known for its surrounding saloons, hotels, bordellos, and warehouses. That bustling center of commerce soon developed into the City of Victoria, and the fort between Wharf and Government Streets became Bastion Square.

Today, this area is known as Old Town. At its center, Bastion Square has evolved from a business hub into a pleasant respite from Victoria's busy thoroughfares. Surrounded by some of the city's oldest nineteenth-century buildings—now housing charming cafés, restaurants, boutiques, offices, and art galleries—the square is a pleasant place to sit and watch the Inner Harbour, picnic, or merely pause from a day's touring. Street performers and bands entertain onlookers while artists at small booths sell their wares.

There's another, more unusual sort of entertainment at Bastion Square as well. The rich history of Old Town has given rise to many tales and legends, and some claim that it is now one of the most haunted parts of Victoria. John Adams, one of Victoria's foremost historians and story-tellers, observes that "almost every building around the historic square has a ghost or two. The 1889 Supreme Court building, home to the Maritime Museum of British Columbia, is said to be the most haunted of all. It was built on the site of the city's first gallows. Many of the hanged men still lie buried beneath its foundations."

# Beacon Hill Park

Beacon Hill Park has it all: trees, lakes, bridges, fountains, gardens, monuments, and even peacocks. Located along the south shore of Victoria, the 62-acre park's central location has long made it a popular recreational destination. The history of the park begins even before the city: First Nations burial cairns found here testify to its historic significance among Native peoples. The area was originally called *Meeacan*, Coast Salish for "belly," because the hilly area looked like the belly of a man lying on his back. The English name for the park refers to a pair of masts that the Hudson's Bay Company placed on Brotchie Ledge in 1843 to act as a beacon to approaching mariners.

Victoria's love for Beacon Hill Park dates back to 1858, when Governor James Douglas set the area aside for public use. In the early years, the City Council banned gambling, shooting, carpet cleaning, and cattle grazing in the park. Visitors to Beacon Hill today still refrain from those activities, engaging in more agreeable ones like walking, bird watching, horseback riding, and beach sports. Endangered Garry oaks flourish in the park amid arbutus, Douglas firs, and western red cedars. Bald eagles nest in the trees, and great blue herons stalk the lakes. The park's natural beauty has attracted many artists, including Victoria's own Emily Carr.

# Inner Harbour

O n Sunday morning, April 25, 1858, life changed abruptly for the 450 inhabitants of Victoria when a side-wheel American steamer, the *Commodore*, entered the Inner Harbour. Within minutes, hundreds of men poured off the deck before the eyes of curious church-going citizens. This vanguard of the Fraser River Gold Rush was followed by 20,000 more men within a few weeks. As the main port of entry, the quiet backwater of Victoria exploded with activity—and was never the same again.

Located near the British Columbia (B.C.) Parliament Buildings and the Fairmont Empress Hotel, the Inner Harbour has always been the ideal place for boaters to get the feel of traditional Victoria. Today it is Victoria's historic center, where hanging flower baskets and a "Welcome to Victoria" sign written in flowers express the city's love of blossoms. A mix of private yachts, commercial fishing boats, public ferries, tour boats, kayaks, and seaplanes float in and out of the harbor. Pedestrians stroll the stone causeway and the stone-walled promenade below it, where artisans and artists display their creations. Others picnic, eat ice cream, and enjoy the music and entertainment of local street performers. Night views in the harbor are particularly pretty, with glowing sidewalk nightlights and the reflection of more than 3,300 light bulbs on the B.C. Parliament Buildings.

Not surprisingly, this delightful atmosphere draws 3.65 million overnight visitors a year, an influx that would surely leave those early church-goers gasping in disbelief. On Belleville and Government Streets adjacent to the Inner Harbour, horse-drawn carriages and double-decker buses serve these visitors. Also conveniently located on the harbor, the Visitor Information Centre on Wharf Street provides hundreds of free brochures as well as hotel and tour bookings.

*Inner Harbour with B.C. Parliament Buildings in background.*

# Victoria Chinatown

At the intersection of Fisgard and Douglas Streets, the ornate Gate of Harmonious Interest, known as Tong Ji Men in Chinese, leads into the oldest existing Chinatown in Canada. Victoria's tiny, two-block Chinatown once supported the largest Chinese settlement north of San Francisco, with trading companies, benevolent societies, tea houses, temples, theaters, churches, a hospital, three schools, and nefarious brothels.

Chinese immigrants arrived on the West Coast of Canada in the mid-1800s. Most came north from San Francisco, lured by the Fraser River Gold Rush of 1858. Within five years, more than 4,000 were working in the Cariboo gold fields. Other Chinese found themselves running laundries and restaurants, growing vegetables, building roads, toiling as houseboys, or canning fish. Later, from 1881 to 1885, some 17,000 Chinese arrived to build the Canadian Pacific Railway—more than 600 of them died in accidents or from the primitive living conditions at the construction sites.

Once the railway to Vancouver was completed, racism against the Chinese grew, and more than 24 anti-Chinese laws were introduced to restrict their rights and freedoms. By the turn of the century, harsh immigration laws prevented their wives and families in China from joining them in Canada. Immigrants were charged a head tax—first of $50, later of $500—to enter the country. Life in British Columbia was a fragile and lonely existence for a Chinese laborer. The gambling dens and thriving opium industry of Chinatown's Fan Tan Alley, reputed to be the narrowest street in Canada, was the only refuge of this "bachelor society." The area was known as "the Forbidden City" by the populace of the day.

Today, Chinatown is a designated heritage area that is home to restaurants, groceries, artists' studios, souvenir shops, and the oldest Buddhist temple in Canada, the 1876 Tam Kung Temple on Government Street. The Gate of Harmonious Interest, built to symbolize the modern spirit of cooperation between the two cultures—Chinese and Western—that created the city of Victoria, was officially dedicated on November 15, 1981. Hand-carved stone lions from Suzhou, Victoria's sister city in China, stand guard on either side of the gate. This grand entryway and exit to the historic neighborhood remains a stark reminder of Victoria's racist past, as well as visual proof of its thriving multicultural present.

*Victoria Chinatown's Gate of Harmonious Interest.*

# Fisgard Lighthouse National Historic Site of Canada

Eight miles from downtown Victoria, Fisgard Lighthouse sits at the entrance to Esquimalt Harbour on tiny Fisgard Island, which was once separate from the mainland but is now connected by a causeway. Creation of a new lighthouse was intended to accommodate increased coastal traffic brought by the Gold Rush of 1858, but paperwork traveling back and forth from England slowed down construction. After two years, it finally opened on November 16, 1860—but the Gold Rush had already slowed to a trickle. Despite its late start, the quaint white tower is still the oldest permanent lighthouse in British Columbia.

John Wright, a Victoria contractor, built the 49-foot-tall tower using only local materials, except for a few large items. The spiral staircase, for example, was cast to his design in San Francisco and shipped north by sea. At the top of the brick tower is an iron-and-glass lantern that was manufactured in England and brought around Cape Horn by sailing ship. Its original lens and lamp could send a beam 10 miles across the Strait of Juan de Fuca.

The adjoining two-story, red-brick house was home to the lighthouse keeper and his family. The lighthouse was run by a series of keepers for many decades, until automation rendered their occupation obsolete in 1929. The former keeper's residence is now a museum commemorating West Coast shipwrecks and the isolated men who tried valiantly to prevent them. Wildlife around the lighthouse is worth a visit in itself: bald eagles, blue herons, and harlequin and eider ducks are frequent flyers here, and otters, harbor seals, and the occasional sea lion can also be spotted.

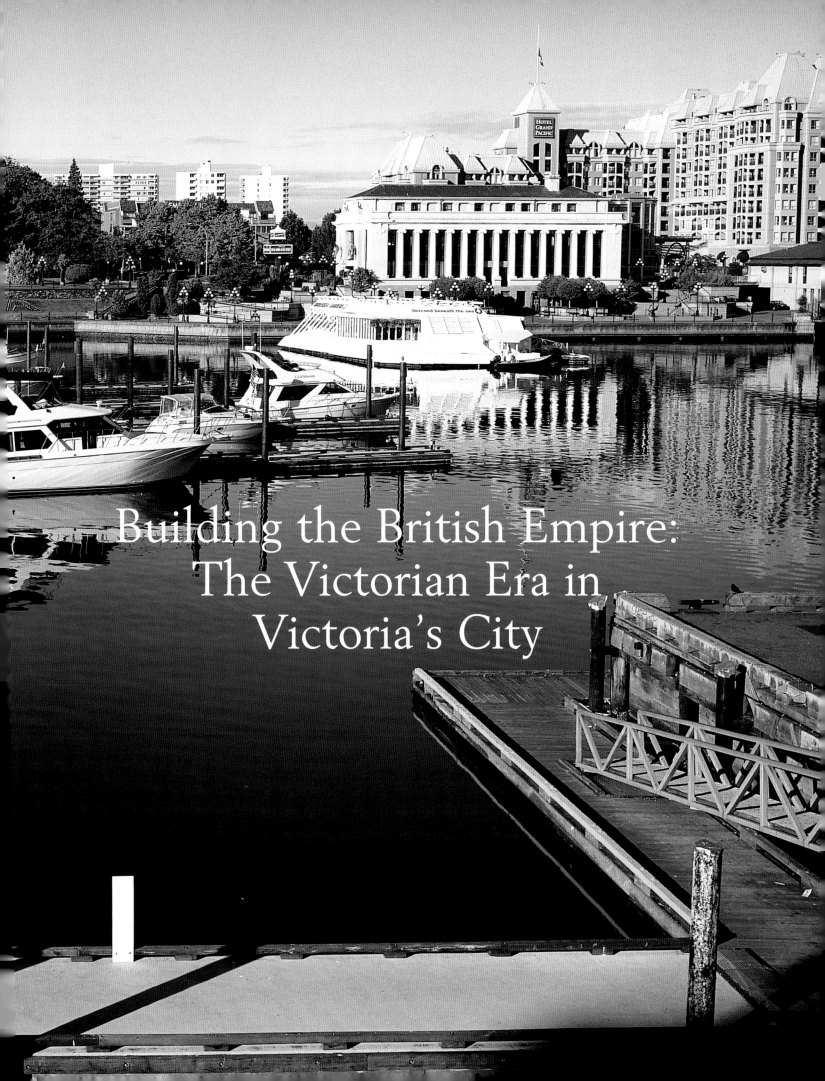

# Building the British Empire: The Victorian Era in Victoria's City

## Queen Victoria Statue

All of Victoria mourned the passing of beloved Queen Victoria on January 22, 1901. The city had been named in her honor, and its citizens celebrated her birthday every year. Born in 1819, Queen Victoria had the longest reign in British history: 63 years, seven months, and two days. In 1887, exuberant festivities had been held in Beacon Hill Park for her jubilee (fiftieth) year anniversary as monarch. When she died, the British Columbia (B.C.) Parliament Buildings were draped in black for her memorial service; the banner above the arched entranceway affirmed "Loved and Mourned by All."

It is fitting that a commemorative bronze statue of Queen Victoria reigns in front of the same buildings. Thirteen feet tall atop a pedestal of granite and Swedish blue marble, the middle-aged queen gazes down with gravity and kindness on her subjects. British Columbia premier Richard McBride commissioned the statue on June 16, 1912. It was designed and executed by British artist Albert Bruce-Joy, who modeled it after a Franz Xaver Winterhalter portrait of Queen Victoria in Buckingham Palace. The statue took some time getting to Victoria: it was not until April 18, 1921, that the finished monument was unveiled before enthusiastic crowds in the queen's namesake city.

*Previous page: View of Victoria B.C. Parliament Buildings across Inner Harbour.*

# Emily Carr House

"The house was large and well-built, the garden prim and carefully tended. Everything about it was extremely English. It was as if Father had buried a tremendous homesickness in this new soil and it had rooted and sprung up English. There were hawthorn hedges, primrose banks, and cow pastures with shrubberies." This is how Emily Carr, a celebrated writer and Canada's most famous female artist, recalled her family home at 207 Government Street in James Bay, where she was born in 1871. Although the home was only a few blocks from the Inner Harbour, the setting was still very rural at that time.

The Carr House was owned by members of Emily's family from 1863 to 1936, then sold to other private owners. In the 1970s, it was taken over and restored by the Province of British Columbia, and is now operated as a museum. The genteel residence is typical of a middle-class family of the Victorian era. Its elegant architecture has been described both as San Francisco Victorian and English Gingerbread. Emily's writings in her senior years provided the renovators with vivid descriptions to follow while refurnishing, and both the house and garden now accurately reflect the home Emily so loved in her youth.

*Helmcken Mausoleum.*

# Ross Bay Cemetery

Ross Bay was named for Isabella Ross, who bought this land in the 1850s. Ross Bay Cemetery off of Dallas Road clings to the bay, making it one of the most beautiful in Canada. The first person buried here was Mary Laetitia Pearse, whose death in December 1872 preceded the official opening by several months. Some 28,000 deceased have followed her to the 27.5-acre historic site. The grounds are an excellent example of a Victorian-era romantic cemetery, with paved carriageways that curve through a landscape of unique trees and plants. A wealth of well-preserved marble, sandstone, and granite tablets, headstones, columns, obelisks, and monuments crowd the site. The site's shady walkways are an ideal place for peaceful contemplation.

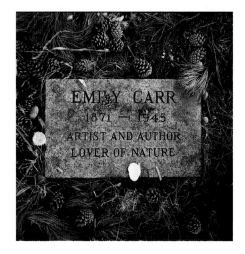

Ross Bay Cemetery holds a veritable who's who of Victoria's past. Wealthy coal baron Robert Dunsmuir lies here, along with groundbreaking local nature artist Emily Carr and notorious prospector Billy Barker of Gold Rush fame. Some, like wealthy politician and society leader Henry (Harry) Dallas Helmcken, rest within family mausoleums. Sir James Douglas, the first governor of British Columbia, is also buried in Ross Bay Cemetery, along with many other premiers. The most unusual of all is Amor De Cosmos, the province's second premier. Born William Alexander Smith in Nova Scotia in 1825, he changed his name to Amor De Cosmos, or "Lover of the Universe." He was premier from 1872 to 1874, went insane in 1895, and died in 1897.

One early giant who also rests here is Sir Matthew Baillie Begbie, the Colony of British Columbia's only judge when he arrived in 1858. Although known as "the Hanging Judge," Begbie did not have much choice: by law, murder was punishable by hanging. He was actually quite merciful: of 52 murder cases, he sentenced only 27 to die. The imposing 6'4"-tall judge, with white hair and black moustache, was sympathetic to the Coast Salish people, who called him "Big Chief." All of Victoria came out for Sir Matthew's funeral procession in 1894. His simple epitaph reads "Lord be Merciful to Me a Sinner."

# Dallas Road

"Dallas Road was the first pleasure drive made in Victoria. Everyone drove along it to admire the view," wrote Victoria artist Emily Carr around the turn of the century. Dallas Road is still a favorite pleasure drive today. Beginning at the Ogden Point Breakwater, the road curves along the south shore of the Strait of Juan de Fuca past Holland Point Park. The view extends as far south as Port Angeles in Washington State and includes the snowcapped peaks of Olympic National Park. On stormy days, people visit the many viewpoints to watch the winds propel waves over the road.

The Ogden Point Breakwater was built between 1913 and 1917 to protect the port of Victoria. The 2,500-foot-long structure is set on a foundation of 65,000 tons of grey granite blocks. A lighthouse at the foot of the breakwater guides cruise ships to the protected side of the port. The outer breakwater is one of Canada's most popular dive spots, where anemones, bull kelp, wolf-eels, octopi, and a multitude of rockfish live to depths of 90 feet.

Two historic cemeteries are found along Dallas Road: Ross Bay Cemetery, the resting place of many famous British Columbians, and the Chinese Cemetery. The latter opened in 1903 at rocky Harling Point on land bought by the Chinese Consolidated Benevolent Association to bury their community's dead with dignity. According to Chinese rites, the deceased were exhumed seven years after death, their bones cleaned and dried and sent back for reburial in China. In 1933, this practice ended; the last burial in the Chinese cemetery was in 1961. About 400 identified people are buried here, but 13 mass graves contain the unmarked remains of another 900 immigrants. In 1996, the Chinese Cemetery was designated a National Historic Site of Canada. A few gravestones marked with Chinese script still stand, along with the twin towers of a ceremonial altar. A revitalization project is gradually transforming the old cemetery into a more park-like setting.

*View of Ross Bay from Dallas Road.*

# Craigdarroch Castle

Wealth and ostentation are evident in every stone of Craigdarroch Castle, built on the highest point in Victoria at 1050 Joan Crescent. What is not evident is the unhappiness of the family that once lived behind its portals. Ironically, perhaps, the name of the home is Gaelic for "rocky oak place."

Craigdarroch was a gift from Scottish coal baron Robert Dunsmuir to his wife Joan and their 11 children, completed shortly after his death in 1889. Dunsmuir, the province's first millionaire, left the bulk of his estate to his eldest son James, but all of his company shares and voting rights to Joan. Thus ensued a decade-long battle between mother and son, with Joan fiercely contesting the will. In 1903, after lengthy and embarrassingly public legal battles, James Dunsmuir was confirmed sole owner of two coal mines, a San Francisco office, a major shareholder in a third mine and in Robert Dunsmuir's Esquimalt & Nanaimo Railway. Sadly, he would never reconcile with his mother, who remained bitter and isolated in her "castle" until her death in 1908.

The estate's original lake, streams, orchard, coach house, stables, and gazebo are long gone. On view today is only the mansion, the south lawn, and an original stone wall. Craigdarroch Castle has seen several incarnations: a military hospital, college campus, music conservatory, and now a tourist attraction. Owned by the City of Victoria, the four-story home with 39 rooms embodies turn-of-the-century elegance, with period furnishings, stained glass windows, a sandstone fireplace, and a grand, white oak staircase. The blue-domed tower room, with its curved doors and circular windows, offers unobstructed views of the Pacific Ocean and the Coast Mountains on the Mainland.

James Dunsmuir followed in his father's footsteps as a successful industrialist, but his reputation was marred by his brutal labor practices: his mines were infamous as the most dangerous in the world. Although he disliked political life, he was premier of the Province of British Columbia from 1900 to 1902 and lieutenant governor from 1906 to 1909. He retired from public life in 1912 at the age of 61, and died at his summer home at Cowichan in 1920.

*Knowledge Totem standing proud on the front lawn of the British Columbia (B.C.) Parliament Buildings.*

# British Columbia (B.C.) Parliament Buildings

After British Columbia joined Canada in 1871, local politicians were determined that Victoria would remain the provincial capital. To aid their campaign, they resolved to create new legislative buildings that would be conspicuous in their grandeur. The prized commission was awarded to Francis Mawson Rattenbury, a young Englishman from Leeds. Rattenbury not only built sumptuous buildings: he completed them for less than $1 million. Construction began in 1892 and was finished five years later. The project's completion was celebrated with a party that drew thousands. Patriotic anthems were sung, military bands played, prayers were offered, and an impressive fireworks display wrapped up the festivities.

Located on Belleville Street, across from The Fairmont Empress Hotel, the buildings feature Neo-Classical elements, such as a copper dome which is now graced with a statue of Captain George Vancouver. Romanesque influences included the use of massive stonework from local quarries. Other local materials were used, notably roofing slate from Jervis Inlet off Vancouver Island. Carved faces and strange gargoyles ornament the building. Inside, the assembly hall features Italian marble, with Tennessee marble in the rotunda.

In 1897, to honor Queen Victoria's sixtieth year on the throne, the central building was outlined with thousands of tiny electric lights. After that time, they were turned on for special occasions only, but due to their popularity they became a nightly tradition in 1956. Now, more than 3,300 bulbs shine brightly every night from dusk till midnight.

# Fort Rodd Hill National Historic Site of Canada

The bleak, concrete-bunkered gun batteries of Fort Rodd Hill attest to its history as an artillery fort. They were built in 1895 to protect the nearby Esquimalt Naval Base and the city of Victoria 8.4 miles away. State-of-the-art artillery enabled Rodd Hill's batteries to attain a gun range of 10,000 yards into the Strait of Juan de Fuca. When the fort closed for active duty in 1956, its guns had—thankfully—never been fired except in practice.

Fort Rodd reopened in 1962 as a National Historic Site of Canada. The 44-acre site today includes a spacious park and three batteries: the Upper Battery, with military paraphernalia representative of the late 1890s; the Lower Battery, with objects from the 1920 to 1939 period; and the Belmont Battery, an anti-torpedo boat battery that has been restored to World War II conditions. The latter features British-built Duplex, or twin, guns from World War II that may be the last of their kind in existence.

Visitors to the fort are not just military buffs. Many come for the park's serene beauty and unique wildlife. Columbian blacktail deer graze the grounds amid Douglas firs, Garry oaks, arbutus, and western red cedar. These small deer, native to British Columbia, are only found in a narrow strip of land along the Pacific coast. From the batteries above or the Fisgard Lighthouse on the shore below, the expansive view of the Strait of Juan de Fuca remains as breathtaking today as it was in the late 1800s.

# Fairmont Empress Hotel

The Fairmont Empress Hotel, architect Francis Mawson Rattenbury's grand lady, shares her fair attributes with a chain of Canadian Pacific Railway (CPR) château-style luxury hotels, including one in Vancouver and another in Whistler. The Empress opened in 1908 at a cost of $1 million, financed by the ever-ambitious railway. It was an instant success: wealthy visitors from Eastern Canada and elsewhere flocked to the British Columbia backwater on board the CPR just to stay in the magnificent edifice.

The hotel's location reflects the railway's power and influence. Surrounded by fragrant gardens and cooling trees, the eight-story-high Empress presides over the Inner Harbour, with the B.C. Parliament Buildings to its left and the business district to its right. An elegant reminder of the Edwardian era, Rattenbury's design combines elements of Gothic, Jacobean, and Elizabethan styles. With its towering brick walls covered in ivy, grand lobby, soaring columns, polished hardwood floors, and antique oak and leather furniture, the Fairmont Empress is one of Victoria's best-loved buildings and the most-photographed of all the city's landmarks. The hotel has been rated one of the top three hotels in North America and number 35 in the world. Not surprisingly, it has seen its share of royalty and celebrity guests. As one gentleman remarked, looking up at the hotel's name above the entrance, "Anyone who doesn't know this is the Empress shouldn't be staying here."

# Butchart Gardens

The Butchart Gardens are the embodiment of the creativity of an orphan, Jeanette Foster Kennedy, born in Toronto in 1868. Despite her sad childhood, the artistic and clever young woman was not destined for tragedy. In 1885, she happily married Robert Pim (Bob) Butchart, an entrepreneur from Ontario. By 1904, the couple had moved to Tod Inlet on Vancouver Island, 13 miles north of Victoria. The property included a rock quarry, where Bob Butchart established the Vancouver Portland Cement Company.

Jennie's initial gardening efforts were spent on beautifying the family garden, but they grew

*Right: Ross Fountain.*

sides of the quarry in a bosun's chair to insert ivy into the crevices.

More than one million bedding plants in 700 varieties blossom every year in the garden's meticulously tended 55 acres, which include the Sunken Garden, the Japanese Garden, the Rose Garden, the Italian Garden, the Concert Lawn, Ross Fountain, and many other smaller areas. On summer nights and during the Christmas season, thousands of lights add a sparkling beauty, powered by one of the largest underground wiring systems in North America at the time of its installation. The gardens remain proudly family-owned, now run by the Ross' great-grand-daughter Robin Clarke. Visitors are free to stroll amid the flowers at their leisure, and more than half a million delight in doing so every year.

into an enduring passion. In 1910, a comment from a friend—"Even you would be unable to get anything to grow in there"—led her to tackle her husband's abandoned limestone quarry, creating what became known as the Sunken Garden. The indomitable Mrs. Butchart, now in her forties, hung down the

*Old Town: Wood-block paving on this turn-of-the-century street leads to the Dominion Drapers Building (1903) and its fine stock of apparel.*

# The Royal British Columbia Museum

The importance of British Columbia's aboriginal and natural heritages were recognized in 1886 by a group of 30 leading Victoria businessmen. On January 16, they asked Lieutenant-Governor Clement F. Cornwall to establish a museum to "preserve specimens of the natural products and Indian antiquities and manufactures of the Province and to classify and exhibit the same for the information of the public." The request was swiftly granted. The new Provincial Museum opened on December 2, 1886 in a small room in the Government Buildings, near today's Royal British Columbia Museum at the corner of Belleville and Government Streets. The museum moved three times before it finally opened in this 26,000-square-foot building, its first permanent home.

A significant decision was made in 1922 to hire a First Nations person, George Hunt of Fort Rupert Reservation, to work with the museum. Hunt was charged with reviewing the Kwakiutl specimens, "in order to have reliable data and information at first hand for the labels." He also provided "the Indian names of many of the plants that are used by the Indians for food and medicine." Today, the Royal British Columbia Museum is respected internationally for its long involvement with First Nations art and culture. A staff of more than 130 full-time employees as well as hundreds of volunteers manages the museum's more than seven million artifacts.

Four galleries in the 26,000-square-foot building display original artifacts in realistic, walk-through scenarios. The newest gallery, "Living Land, Living Sea," focuses on climate change; the Gallery of Natural History introduces B.C.'s forests and ocean and the history of settlement; the First Peoples Gallery includes early photographs, video, and audio; and the Modern History Gallery takes visitors on a recreated journey through the streets of nineteenth-century Victoria. The museum is also home to the National Geographic IMAX Theatre, with a six-story screen that shows giant documentaries in air-conditioned comfort.

*First Peoples Gallery: The pole in the right foreground was part of a house frame in the village of Tanu on Haida Gwaii (Queen Charlotte Islands).*

# Thunderbird Park

Thunderbird Park, at the corner of Douglas and Belleville Streets, owes its existence to a collection of neglected old totem poles that had been stored in a drill hall on nearby Menzies Street. In 1940, concerned citizens anxious to preserve remnants of what was believed to be a dying culture raised the poles on a vacant lot next to the Provincial Museum (now the Royal British Columbia Museum). The "Model Indian Village" was opened by Premier T. D. Patullo and Victoria mayor Andrew McGavin.

In 1952, the decaying poles inspired the government to hire renowned Kwakwaka'wakw carver Chief Mungo Martin as head carver of a totem restoration program. In 1962, after Martin's death, his successor Henry Hunt

stepped in, followed by Richard Hunt and Tim Paul. Many skilled carvers, including Doug Cranmer, Bill Reid, Gerry Marks, and Simon Charlie, have worked here in the past, and Native carvers still serve as resident artists in the park's Carving Studio. These days, rather than dying out, Native carving has taken on an informed presence, with knowledgeable and talented artists continuing their traditions—partially thanks to the creation of Thunderbird Park.

More than a dozen carved poles now stand in Thunderbird Park. They include examples of coastal Native works, including Kwakwaka'wakw heraldic poles and a house post, Gitxsan memorial poles, Nuxalk grave figures, Haida memorial and mortuary poles, and a Cumshewa pole. There is also a Kwakwaka'wakw-style building known as the Mungo Martin House, with the face of a giant green sea monster in the form of a spiny fish called a sculpin painted across the front. Visitors are invited into the Carving Studio to watch the carvers work, ask them questions, and even purchase their art.

*Above: Ming Dynasty Chinese bell.*

*Below: Entrance Hall.*

# Art Gallery of Greater Victoria

The Art Gallery of Greater Victoria is partially housed in Gyppeswick, a historic family mansion at 1040 Moss Street. The home was built in 1889 by David Spencer, a Welshman who moved to Victoria in 1862 and opened a chain of David Spencer Ltd. department stores. In 1951, the house was donated to the City of Victoria, which converted its tall ceilings, original

*The Art Gallery of Greater Vancouver's Shinto shrine is the only authentic Shinto shrine outside of Japan.*

fireplaces, wood moldings, and elegant staircase into the Art Gallery of Greater Victoria.

Victoria's preeminent painter, Emily Carr, is justifiably prominent at the gallery, with six rooms dedicated to permanent exhibitions of her masterworks of the West Coast rainforest. One exhibit introduces this unique woman using historical photographs, examples of her writing, and her dramatic paintings of Coast Salish totem poles and twisted and towering Douglas firs. Not surprisingly, the gallery's collection also reflects the city's long-enduring fascination with Oriental art, which dates back to the Victorian era. Its vast Asian collection is the second largest in Canada, and its collection of Asian lacquer and ivory is one of the finest in all North America. Particularly notable among the many Eastern artifacts is the only authentic Shinto shrine outside of Japan. Other remarkable pieces include a Ming Dynasty bell and the head of a Buddha from the fourteenth century.

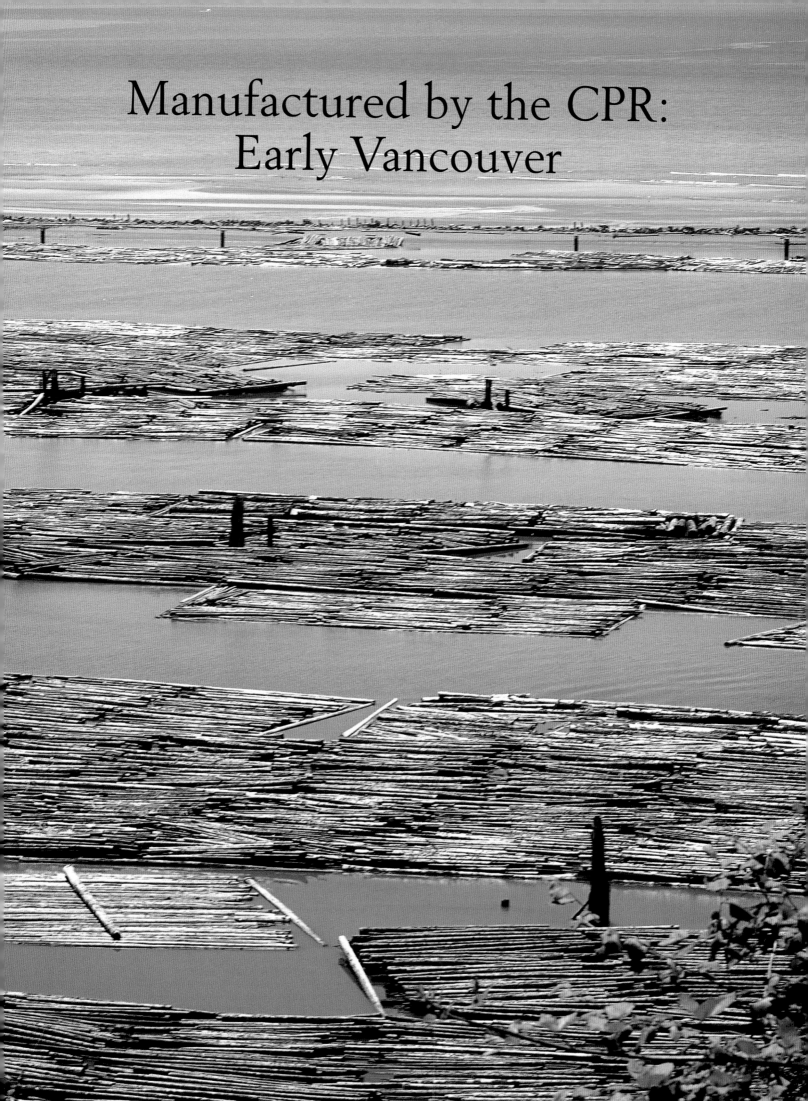

# Manufactured by the CPR:
# Early Vancouver

# The North Shore

Beyond Vancouver lies the North Shore, with its string of 15 mountain peaks nestling around the two urban centers of North Vancouver and West Vancouver. The trip across Burrard Inlet is easy now—not so in the days of ferries, which persisted until the Ironworkers Memorial Bridge (also called the Second Narrows) was built in 1925. In 1938, it was joined over the inlet by the $6 million Lions Gate Bridge, one of Vancouver's two most famous bridges. The affluent Guinness family (of Irish brewing fame) financed construction of the bridge so that potential homebuyers in their posh new West Vancouver housing development would not have to take the ferries to get home. They owned the bridge until 1963, when it was purchased by the province of British Columbia. The bridge features the work of sculptor Charles Marega in the form of two lions at the east entrance. Lions Gate Bridge is one of Vancouver's defining landmarks, and is likely to remain so for generations to come.

The Coast Mountains stretch across the North Shore horizon from Black Mountain in the west to Mt. Seymour in the east. The most recognizable are the side-by-side West and East Lions Peaks, so called because they resemble two resting lions. However, Chief Joe Capilano, a beloved leader of the local Squamish people, had a different name for them: to honor the courage of two sisters who stopped a war between local tribes, the women were turned into the "Two Sisters" Peaks.

*Pages 72–73: View of the Fraser River from Pacific Spirit Regional Park.*

*Opposite: The Coast Mountains overlooking Vancouver's North Shore make for quite a skyline at sunset.*

*Fireworks over West Vancouver celebrate Canada Day.*

Three North Shore mountain areas are popular year-round attractions for mountaineers and skiers. Grouse Mountain is the best-known resort area. Cypress Mountain, located in Cypress Provincial Park, is the largest, encompassing the Hollyburn, Black, and Strachan peaks. Mt. Seymour Provincial Park in North Vancouver includes Mt. Seymour, Mt. Elsay, and Mt. Bishop. Visitors to any of these enjoy breathtaking panoramic views that include towering Mount Baker in the United States. In winter, the North Shore's steep, forested slopes are tinged white by a lacy blanket of snow, creating a distinctive beauty that leaves an indelible impression on visitors. Exclusive homes continue to rise ever higher on the slopes, yet nature remains: black bears, cougars, and coyotes regularly prowl along the edge of habitation.

*Lions Gate Bridge*

# Vancouver International Airport & Public Transit

*Bill Reid's* The Spirit of Haida Gwaii, The Jade Canoe.

Vancouver International Airport (YVR) is located on Sea Island in Richmond, 25 minutes from the city of Vancouver. The first passenger flights from Sea Island were launched in 1932 from a wood frame terminal. Today, YVR is rated one of the top airports in the world, with more than 15.5 million travelers annually passing through its national and international terminals. More than 266,000 flights take off and land each year, making YVR the third largest international passenger gateway on the West Coast of North America.

YVR offers waiting passengers a host of basic as well as luxurious amenities, but what truly lifts it above other airports is its impressive and very visible collection of Canadian art, including world-class First Nations and Inuit art. The most prominent of the original artworks is famed Haida artist Bill Reid's massive bronze cast, *The Spirit of Haida Gwaii, The Jade Canoe*. The monumental sculpture of a canoe is filled with larger-than-life mythological Haida figures. Dramatically set against the backdrop of the glass Wave Wall, the masterpiece is the focal point of the entrance to the international terminal.

Once visitors manage to pull themselves away from the airport's art collection to head into town, they understand very quickly why Greater Vancouver's public transit system has won awards. The system began in 1889 with an argument pitting horse-drawn railway cars against electric-powered ones. Lawyer Henry McKee convinced backers of the Vancouver Street Railways to go with the new-fangled electric trains. The city's horses were sold and six electric rail cars purchased from an American manufacturer. On June 26, 1890, the first electric streetcar out of the barn drew hundreds of onlookers as it made a trial run down Westminster Avenue (now Main Street). Two days later, the 5.9-mile system opened for regular service at five cents a ride.

Now, more than 62 million residents and visitors a year use TransLink, Greater Vancouver's truly groundbreaking public transit system. The service area encompasses 695 square miles and employs a variety of vehicles. In addition to diesel-driven buses, Vancouver has an electric trolley fleet second in size only to that of San Francisco. SkyTrain, one of the world's few elevated light rapid transit systems, has won praise and awards from critics for its beautiful, architecturally unique stations. Spanning the Fraser River is SkyBridge, the world's longest cable-stayed bridge designed solely for rapid transit use, with spectacular views of Washington State's snow-clad Mount Baker on a clear day. Last but not least, the world's first SeaBus ferries make more than 45,000 12-minute trips across Vancouver Bay every year—and with a crew of only four! Four hundred passengers can exit and another 400 board in 90 seconds; in three minutes, SeaBus is on its way again.

*Gastown Steam Clock*

## Gastown

In the early days of Vancouver, eccentric characters such as Captain John "Gassy Jack" Deighton appeared as if out of nowhere, made their mark, and then faded into history. A Yorkshireman, Gassy Jack (so called because he was always talking) arrived at Burrard Inlet in the fall of 1867 with his Native wife and dog and opened the Globe Saloon. As the first settler in the area, Gassy Jack would lend his name to Gastown, around which the new town of Granville—later Vancouver—began to grow. In his honor, a statue of the inimitable saloon keeper has been erected on Maple Tree Square, looking west along Water Street.

With only a transient population of lumbermen, mill workers, sailors, and whalers, the area became a hodgepodge of hotels, saloons, and grocery stores, but very few homes. After it was announced that Gastown would be the terminus of the new transcontinental railway, however, the permanent population would grow from only 75 residents in 1873 to 3,000 in 1886. On April 6 of that year, the town was officially renamed Vancouver by Canadian Pacific Railway President William Van Horne.

Then came the Great Fire. On June 13, 1886, Vancouver burned to the ground, reduced to ashes and rubble in a few frenzied hours. Before the ashes had even stopped smoldering, however, Vancouver began rebuilding—this time of stone and brick. Many of the imposing structures still stand, now housing souvenir shops, art galleries, boutiques, and a variety of other businesses. Gastown's revival was given a boost in 1971 when its was designated a historic district by the Province of British Columbia.

Public clockmaker Raymond Saunders' Gas-town Steam Clock on the corner of Water and Cambie Streets is one of the area's main attractions, especially for tourists. Built in 1977, the clock is not a historic artifact, but its movements are based on an 1875 design. Powered by a continuous supply of steam from a steam vent beneath the street, the clock has had to release internal pressure every 15 minutes of every day since it was dedicated on September 24, 1977—by letting off a fun, sometimes surprising, hiss of steam.

*Statue of Captain John "Gassy Jack" Deighton on Maple Tree Square.*

*An Inuksuk—a stone sculpture used by Inuit people as a landmark in their travels—stands near Second Beach.*

## West End

The West End is Canada's most densely populated square kilometer. In spite of its high traffic, the presence of English Bay and the proximity of Stanley Park have a calming effect on visitors and residents. Vintage houses and high rises, palm trees and beachfront, seawall strolls and shoreline parks are some of the features that characterize this favorite Vancouver neighborhood.

The West End is historically home to well-off Vancouverites, and many of the area's tightly packed homes, shopfronts, and streets seem to breathe an air of refinement. One of the eight turn-of-the century heritage homes on Barclay Heritage Square, the 1893 Roedde House, is another of famed architect Francis Mawson Rattenbury's Vancouver masterpieces. Robson Street, once dubbed "Robsonstrasse" for its German cafés, has blossomed into a mecca for international shoppers looking for the latest fashions. The street's up-scale boutiques, ethnic restaurants, and specialty coffee shops teem with customers. Since 1890, Second Beach has been the ultimate West End destination for those who wish to see and be seen. The long stretch of sand along the bay includes Sunset and Third Beaches as well. All three beaches are

*Sunset Beach*

*Second Beach*

linked by a wide seawall walk built on land reclaimed from the sea. In 1987, an Inuksuk (an ancient symbol of Inuit culture used as a landmark in northern travels) was added to the atmosphere. The rough-hewn, human-like figure stands along the beach, its arms open in a friendly gesture to passers-by.

Hiking along a wind-swept beach is a popular West Coast activity—even cold and rain does not stop most Vancouver beach walkers. All the city's dozen beaches have several characteristics in common: all are open to swim-mers, all (with the exception of Wreck Beach) have lifeguards, and all are bordered by walking paths. Each beach has its own style, however, attracting sometimes very different crowds: English Bay attracts mostly families out for a day of picnicking, as do the park-like atmospheres of Spanish Banks and Locarno Beach. Kitsilano Beach is known for its youthful crowd and free evening entertainment. Jericho Beach attracts windsurfers, sunbathers, and the annual Vancouver International Folk Music Festival.

Vancouver's beaches have long been a barometer of change. As the first city historian, Major J. S. Matthews, recalled of English Bay around 1906, women swam wearing neck-to-knee bathing suits accessorized with stock-ings and shoes until "...one impertinent hussy, bolder than the others, went in bathing without her stockings. She was a sight to behold—she was bare naked right up to her knees." Nowadays, Wreck Beach, below a steep, wooded hill on the University of British Columbia site, is clothing-optional. In spite of its notoriety, the majority of Vancouverites have never visited it.

*Second Beach*

## Fraser River

"As truly as the gold bars, the sedimentary rock and the delta, Vancouver is a conglomerate mixed by the Fraser's current.... By the little measure of men's affairs, Vancouver is the river's masterpiece," wrote historian Bruce Hutchison in his book *The Fraser*. Before that masterpiece was built, the same river supported Native habitation for more than 10,000 years. It inspired the first major influx of Europeans during the Gold Rush of 1858. In the 1880s and '90s, salmon canneries proliferated where the river met the Pacific. The Fraser is the largest salmon river in the world, notable for its sockeye salmon runs in particular, but countless other animals and plants also live in its estuary and delta. Forestry is the leading industry along the river; shipping and related industries now employ more than 100,000 people. Half of British Columbia's population live in cities and towns along its banks.

The majestic Fraser River travels 850 miles south from its birthplace in Fraser Pass, a remote corner of Mt. Robson Provincial Park. Growing powerful and dangerous, it traverses the narrow Fraser Canyon at Hell's Gate, widens at Hope, and passes through the Fraser Valley's rich farmlands until arriving at its estuary—Vancouver—where it splits into north and south arms, creating two separate ports for the city. Simon Fraser was the first European to travel the river's length in 1808, and, despite the fact that he disliked the river that nearly killed him on multiple occasions, it was named after him.

# Vancouver's Chinatown

*Dr. Sun Yat-Sen Classical Chinese Garden*

The roots of Vancouver's Chinatown date back to the 1880s, when more than 17,000 Chinese immigrants came to what they called "Saltwater City" to build the Canadian Pacific Railway. After the railway reached Vancouver, Chinese workers found themselves unemployed, destitute, and mostly without family support due to Canada's racist immigration laws. They lived in a miserable, cramped Chinatown on the then-swampy shores of False Creek.

Today's Chinatown couldn't be more different. Bordered by Gore Avenue and Carrall, Pender, and Keefer Streets, the neighborhood is a fascinating mix of shops selling fruits, vegetables, herbal medicines, teas, Chinese souvenirs, and dry goods. Dozens of restaurants offer delicious Chinese regional cuisines. On summer weekends, the night market spills onto streets bustling with locals and tourists. Contrasting starkly with this commotion is the serenity of Dr. Sun Yat-Sen Classical Chinese Garden on Carrall Street: the authentic Ming Dynasty garden was the first full-scale Chinese garden built outside of China, and is still one of only two. The residents' once-difficult history is honored throughout the neighborhood: at the Chinese Cultural Centre Museum and Archives, in plaques commemorating early Chinese immigrants, and in the Pender Street Millennium Gate—a powerful symbol of a new era of cooperation and peace.

*One of many aromatic shops selling authentic Chinese fare near Millennium Gate.*

# Yaletown

Vancouver, today's beautiful "City by the Sea," owes its success to the dirt and grime of industry. From the 1880s onward, the shingle mills and sawmills along the misnamed "False Creek"—in reality a tidal basin—belched pollution over the city. After 1887, when the Canadian Pacific Railway (CPR) extended its line from Port Moody to Vancouver, railyards crowded the north shore of False Creek. Crews from the CPR's former base of operations in Yale, B.C. moved in to service the locomotives. Thus "Yaletown" was born.

Warehouses sprung up along Mainland, Homer, and Hamilton Streets. By the 1920s, False Creek's waters were a toxic soup of metals, chemicals, waste, and decay. By the 1950s, many believed the "filthy ditch" should be filled in, but little changed for two more decades. Transformation of the area began in earnest in the 1970s, when a group of determined city planners tackled the south shore with projects such as the Granville Island Market. The north shore and Yaletown didn't get their much-needed attention for another two decades. Their launching pad was Expo 86, Vancouver's hugely successful 1986 world exposition. Built along a narrow, five-mile-long strip on the north shore of False Creek, the

*Sidewalk café in Yaletown.*

*Historic Engine No. 374, on display at Yaletown's CPR Roundhouse.*

Expo grounds bordered on the battered heritage warehouses of Yaletown. Unnoticed for years, the transformation of Yaletown soon began. Chic condominiums, offices, restaurants, cafés, boutiques, and high-tech companies now compete for space in the desirable Yaletown area.

The busy Roundhouse Community Centre on the former Expo 86 site is a meeting place for the area's residents. Next door is the CPR Roundhouse, now an Expo 86 heritage building. Engine No. 374, which pulled the first passenger train into Vancouver in May 1887, has pride of place here as one of Vancouver's designated heritage artifacts.

Yaletown has become one of Vancouver's trendiest neighborhoods, but its heritage has not been obscured. Old warehouses continue to undergo costly renovations instead of being demolished. New owners are preserving a part of Vancouver's industrial heritage that many thought could never be reclaimed—and future owners will surely thank them for it.

*Heritage Hall on Main Street in Mount Pleasant.*

## Mount Pleasant

Overlooking downtown Vancouver, historic Mount Pleasant bustles with antique stores, coffee shops, trendy restaurants, and boutiques featuring the styles of groundbreaking local designers. Back in 1888, the area was far less desirable—in fact, local residents were tired of disparaging remarks made about their working-class neighborhood. When Mrs. Henry Edmonds suggested it be named Mount Pleasant after her birthplace in Ireland, the new name caught on quickly. Mount Pleasant's population, much of which was comprised of immigrants, grew into the multi-cultural community one sees today.

Heritage Hall, an impressive community treasure, presides over Main Street, the central thoroughfare of Mount Pleasant. The hilltop cultural hub is the city's finest example of Beaux Arts Classicism, opened as a post office in 1915.

After stints as a seed-testing lab and a Royal Canadian Mounted Police station and forensic lab, the building was saved from abandonment and decay by the community itself. The designated heritage building was reopened as a community center in 1982.

The impressive building has become a well-loved landmark, noted for its copper roof and stately clock tower, the last working hand-wound clock in Vancouver. Carved exterior details include stern old men, smiling young ladies, and a man in a peaked cap, possibly representing the original postmen. Myths have swirled around the hall over the years: stories of ghosts, strange experiments in its upstairs lab, and caretakers who moonlighted as moonshiners. They may hold little truth, but they do endear the building even more to the residents of Mount Pleasant.

# Shaughnessy

Thomas George Shaughnessy, an American railroad man, was recruited by the Canadian Pacific Railroad (CPR) over a glass of beer in 1882. By 1898, he had risen from general purchasing agent to president of Canada's first transcontinental railway. He was knighted for his efforts in 1901, and became the first Baron Shaughnessy of Montreal in 1916.

Sir Thomas Shaughnessy left an indelible mark on Vancouver. In September 1909, he purchased a building lot from the CPR's land grant holdings and built himself a mansion. The city's elite followed suit—as Shaughnessy knew they would—avidly buying lots on the 6,000-acre hillside overlooking the city. Within a few years, the forested area that had become known as Shaughnessy Heights was home to 243 families, the majority of which were listed in Vancouver's most exclusive social registers.

Shaughnessy's huge vintage homes, tree-lined streets, and Old World charm reflect the pre-World War I "golden age" of Vancouver's wealthiest residents, designed by the province's leading architects. Classic Tudor Revival mansions were the specialty of Victoria architect Samuel Maclure and his Vancouver partner C. C. Fox. Their styles included Spanish Colonial haciendas, huge California bungalows, Cape Cod cottages, and eighteenth-century Georgian townhouses.

Vancouver's most famous unsolved murder took place in Shaughnessy on July 26, 1924. Janet Smith, a 22-year-old Scottish nanny, was found shot to death in the home of F. L. Baker, a wealthy pharmaceuticals exporter. Police first said Smith's death was a suicide or an accident. Eight months later, Wong Foon Sing, the Chinese houseboy who had discovered Smith's body, was abducted and held prisoner in an attic room by a group of vigilantes that included the Point Grey reeve, a police chief, and four constables. Sing was accused of the murder but later acquitted; he returned to China in January 1926. The sensational case remains unsolved.

*"Mansion on the Crescent," Shaughnessy Park.*

*University Women's Club.*

# Granville Island

Granville Island was never a real island. It was originally nothing more than two sandbars used by Coast Salish fishers. In 1915, the Vancouver Harbour Commission expanded the bars into an island for industrial use, and soon the area was choked with sawmills and factories. Rescue came to the toxic mess in 1972 in the form of "The Barefoot Gang," a group of urban planners and architects. Their initiative led to the transformation of industrial Granville Island into a bright and busy marketplace. Ocean Cement is now the only industry operating here amid shops, theaters, art galleries, marinas, offices, artist studios, museums, and residences.

The island is located beneath one of Vancouver's two most famous bridges. The city is criss-crossed by a dozen or so bridges, but the Burrard Street Bridge, erected in 1932, was the first bridge built high enough to allow ships on False Creek to pass under. Several architectural details make it unique: its Art Deco design; its two concrete pillars, which were built twice as large as required to suggest mountains; two small rooms hidden in the arches of the pillars; and the juxtaposition of concrete piers and steel railings to symbolize the bonding of natural and man-made worlds. Noted sculptor Charles Marega designed the city's coat of arms and the busts of Captain George Vancouver and his friend Sir Harry Burrard that are displayed on the bridge.

The island's hub of activity is the huge Granville Island Public Market. Beneath the roof of a converted warehouse, hundreds of sellers display their produce and products daily. Fresh fruit arrives from British Columbia's Okanagan, dairy products from the Fraser Valley, and flowers from local growers. Vendors sell everything from hand-knitted scarves to homemade chocolates. Many of the millions of visitors who come to the island every year come simply as sightseers. They pause to order at the fast-food outlets in the market—with menus that vary

*View of downtown Vancouver from Granville Island*

*Granville Island Public Market*

from hamburgers to Thai hot-and-spicy dishes, Vietnamese wraps, and Greek souvlakis—then share tables with strangers or take their food outside to False Creek to share it with the seagulls. Street performers entertain with guitars, flutes, and accordions, while stand-up comics and magicians attract gathering crowds.

The island is also home to two marinas, water ferries, and an ever-changing mix of activities. One of the island's prominent tenants is the Emily Carr Institute of Art and Design, named after Victoria's most famous artist. The Charles F. Scott Gallery at street level offers the public several new exhibits each year. One of the most delightful features of Granville Island is a children's waterpark with refreshing jets and splash fountains that draw happy crowds on hot summer days. From Granville Island, pedestrians can stroll east along the False Creek seawall to Science World at the far end of the creek, a picturesque, hour-long walk.

*Burrard Street Bridge*

95

# Stanley Park

From any angle, Stanley Park is impressive. It is the third-largest city-owned park in North America, more than twice the size of New York's Central Park. The much-loved 1,000-acre recreation area is located at 2099 Beach Avenue, only a 10-minute bus ride from downtown Vancouver.

Musqueam and Squamish people lived here at a village known as Khwaykhway until, in 1888, they were expelled by the government so that a road could be built through the area. After the "Great Fire" of June 13, 1886 rendered the fledgling city a heap of ashes, elected alderman

*A game of cricket at Stanley Park, along Coal Harbour.*

Girl in Wetsuit, *a 1972 statue by Elek Imredy.*

*Totem Park at Brockton Point.*

Lauchlan Alexander Hamilton suggested taking advantage of the opportunity to build anew by creating a large park on the outskirts of town. A park at the site of the former Native village was approved and, three years later, the Governor General of Canada, Lord Stanley, visited Vancouver to open Stanley Park to all. He vowed that it would be forever dedicated "to the use and enjoyment of people of all colours, creeds and customs for all time." To this day, that promise is honored by more than eight million visitors a year, making Stanley Park Vancouver's top attraction.

A 6.5-mile-long seawall winds around the perimeter of the park, a massive project that was completed in 1980 after more than 60 years of hard labor. The wall winds past Siwash Rock, an ancient volcanic lava formation that juts from the ocean. One legend says the rock was a young Squamish chief who was transformed into enduring stone to honor his courage. Another offshore rock along the wall is occupied by *Girl in Wetsuit*, a 1972 bronze sculpture by Elek Imredy.

Visitors to the park can visit beaches, swimming pools, restaurants and take-away stands, a children's petting zoo, tennis courts, a pitch and putt course, and a rowing and yacht club. Other interesting sites here include the Vancouver Aquarium Marine Science Centre, the musical Theatre Under the Stars at Malkin Bowl, Totem Park at Brockton Point, the 1915 Brockton Point Lighthouse, and the Nine O'Clock Gun, which has been fired nightly at nine o' clock since 1894. In spite of all the cultural and sports activity, Stanley Park's natural beauty remains surprisingly well preserved: it is still as wonderful a place to visit forests, lakes, rolling greens, and high lookout points as it was a century ago.

*View of downtown from Stanley Park.*

*Dolphin show*

# Vancouver Aquarium Marine Science Centre

A 16-foot bronze orca whale makes a dazzling leap in front of the Vancouver Aquarium Marine Science Centre on Avison Way in Stanley Park. Installed in 1984, the sculpture by eminent Haida artist Bill Reid is called *Chief of the Undersea World*. Orcas (or "killer whales," as they are often called) no longer swim in the aquarium's huge pools, but Reid's work still symbolizes the goals of this internationally respected science center.

The aquarium has been part of Vancouver since June 15, 1956, five years after the idea was first conceived by the Vancouver Public Aquarium Association. The facility has grown from 9,000 to 100,000 square feet, and from a staff of twelve to 280. Water habitats feature beluga whales, sea otters, sea lions, seals, dolphins, octopi, and eels. In addition, more than 167 aquatic displays are home to more than 60,000 aquatic creatures. Specific exhibits include Treasures of the British Columbia Coast, Arctic Canada, Clownfish Cove, and Amazon Rain-forest. Sharks are fed in full view of visitors in the Shark Habitat in the Tropic Zone.

The Vancouver Aquarium and Marine Science Centre boasts a virtual grocery list of firsts. It was the first public aquarium in Canada, and the first aquarium in Canada to incorporate professional naturalists on-site. It was the first facility in the world to study a young male orca, named Moby Doll, in July of 1964, and it created the first on-site orca habitat in 1967. In September of 1975, it became the first aquarium to be accredited by the American Association of Zoological Parks and Aquariums (AZA). January 1981 hailed the first birth of a sea otter in an aquarium in Canada. And late in 1996, in response to changing times and values, the Vancouver Aquarium and Marine Science Centre became the first facility in the world to vow never again to capture, or cause to be captured, a wild whale or dolphin. In addition, the aquarium's Marine Mammal Rescue and Rehabilitation Centre has led the way in efforts to save the lives of marine animals for more than four decades, with a success count of more than 2,000 lives to date.

*Beluga whale*

# Queen Elizabeth Park

*Bloedel Floral Conservatory*

Queen Elizabeth Park is located on what locals refer to as Little Mountain, a 505-foot summit that is the highest point in Vancouver. More than six million people visit the 130-acre park every year to enjoy its treed slopes, quarry garden, rose garden, floral conservatory, and fabulous view of the Vancouver skyline.

In 1929, the Vancouver Park Board bought the derelict rock quarry that was Little Mountain and began transforming it into a public park. Ten years later, King George VI and his consort, Queen Elizabeth, dedicated the park amid the fanfare of an adoring public. In the decades since, the park board has worked hard to develop Canada's first civic arboretum, planting specimens of all of Canada's native trees as well as many exotic international species.

In the late 1960s, the park was expanded with a $1.25 million donation from Washingtonian Prentice Bloedel, the soft-spoken president of one of the West Coast's biggest logging and saw milling companies—as well as a passionate gardener. Bloedel's donation to Queen Elizabeth Park was used to build Canada's first geodesic conservatory, the Bloedel Floral Conservatory, opened on December 6, 1969. Inside the climate-controlled dome, several zones present tropical, desert, and exotic plants, as well as more than 100 free-flying birds.

# VanDusen Botanical Garden

The VanDusen Botanical Garden began life in 1912 as the Shaughnessy Heights Golf Course, Vancouver's first full-length golflinks. In 1960, the golf course moved to a new location, and for a time it looked as if the property might become a housing development. Then a group of local citizens stepped in and formed the VanDusen Botanical Garden Association, named for local lumber magnate and philanthropist, Whitford Julian VanDusen. The association worked with the Vancouver Park Board to save the land and transform it into a botanical garden, a $3 million undertaking that was financed by the Province of British Columbia, the City of Vancouver, and VanDusen himself.

On August 30, 1975, the 55-acre VanDusen Botanical Garden opened to the public. Vancouver's mild climate enables the growth of more than 7,500 varieties of flowers, plants, shrubs, and trees from six continents, many of which were planted with the region's four distinct seasons in mind in order to create ever-changing displays of color. Special gardens take advantage of rolling lawns, peaceful lakes, artistic rockwork, and forested expanses. The site also contains theme areas, such as the Canadian Heritage Garden, Chinese Medicinal Garden, Children's Garden, Fragrance Garden, Meditation Garden, Rose Garden, Sino-Himalayan Garden, the Rhododendron Walk, and a fern dell—there's even a maze! The gardens hold many annual special events, the most prominent of which are the Christmas Festival of Lights, the April plant sale, and an always-sold-out flower and garden show in June.

# Museum of Anthropology

*Left: Totem poles in the museum's Great Hall.*

*Right:* Raven and the First Men, *a yellow cedar carving by West Coast Native artist Bill Reid.*

A rich heritage of First Nations cultures and traditions makes the West Coast unique. To preserve examples of these ancient cultures, the University of British Columbia's Museum of Anthropology (MOA), founded in 1949, houses a research collection of some 230,000 artifacts. MOA includes an extensive group of Kwakwaka'wakw, Nisga'a, Gitksan, Haida, and Coast Salish household and artistic objects that is undoubtedly one of the finest collections of Northwest Coast First Nations art in the world.

As visitors explore the museum, they discover a display system known as "visible storage." More than 90 percent of the collection is kept in glass-topped drawers, accessible to the public. The museum's use of both natural light and visible storage met with controversy when the museum opened in 1976; since then, UBC's system has become the model for many other museums.

West Coast art is often thought of solely in terms of totem poles and cedar canoes. At MOA, however, it is evident that Native artists also worked in smaller dimensions, including dance masks, cooking boxes, feast bowls, and exquisitely carved jewelry and miniature sculptures of argillite, silver, gold, and bone. The museum features outdoor as well as indoor exhibits: looking out to the Pacific Ocean are two Haida houses designed by Bill Reid and Doug Cranmer and a collection of modern totem poles carved by some of the coast's best-known Native artists.

The resurgence of coastal Native art is a powerful indication that these cultures have not only survived, but are thriving once again. Haida artist Bill Reid was one of the first to revive the ancient skills in modern times. One of Reid's large-scale masterpieces, *Raven and the First Men,* is on display at the museum. Carved in yellow cedar, the work portrays the Haida legend of the trickster Raven discovering the first humans in a clamshell.

# Vancouver Museum

The Vancouver Museum opened in 1968 on the south shore of False Ceek near the Burrard Bridge, but it dates back to the mid-1880s, when it began life in a rented room on Granville Street. The museum's building in Vanier Park is notable for its white roof, which resembles a woven hat worn by early Coast Salish people. It is perhaps symbolic of the Native roots of the park, where Sun'ahk Squamish Indians once made their home: In the early 1800s, Chupkheem of Sun'ahk (also known as Chief George) left his village on the Squamish River to build a home and large potlatch house here. The area was an Indian Reserve until logging, settlement, and the Canadian Pacific Railway encroached on the territory in the 1880s.

Since the museum's first donation—a stuffed trumpeter swan—it has grown so large that a good portion of its collection has to be stored in a football field-sized storage vault in the basement. Many of the exhibits feature local history, including permanent walk-through displays that take viewers from a fur-trading post to the steerage bunks of an immigrant ship. The glory days of Vancouver's timber industry are portrayed, as is Gastown's motley crew of ne'er-do-well mariners. Gentility finally comes to the Vancouver Museum in the form of an Edwardian household, complete with parlor, bedroom, kitchen, and pantry.

The building's entrance is adorned by George Norris' huge stainless steel sculpture, *The Crab*, one of the most-photographed of Vancouver's many sculptural treasures. The museum's foyer is also the entrance to the H. R. MacMillan Space Centre, opened in October 1997 and named for lumber magnate Harvey Reginald MacMillan. Nearby is the H. R. MacMillan Planetarium, which was donated by MacMillan himself in 1967, Canada's centennial year, as a gift to the City of Vancouver. Multimedia shows are presented in the planetarium's renovated Star Theatre using large-format video with new

*Above: The Coast Salish hat-like roof of the Vancouver Museum.*

*Below: George Norris' stainless steel sculpture,* The Crab.

*Chung Hung's red steel sculpture,* Gate to the North-West Passage, *frames English Bay.*

laser projection and other technological enhancements.

The 37-acre Vanier Park surrounding the museum was named for Georges P. Vanier, governor general of Canada from 1959 until his death in 1967. The largely tree-less expanse is a favorite of kite flyers, who take advantage of the breezes that swoosh in unhindered from English Bay. A massive red steel sculpture by Chung Hung called *Gate to the North-West Passage* breaks the grassy plain near the water's edge. In May, Vanier Park is home to the annual Vancouver International Children's Festival.

# Vancouver Art Gallery

The Vancouver Art Gallery bears the signature of the province's best known early architect, Englishman Francis Mawson Rattenbury, whose first commission in Canada was a prestigious project in Victoria: the B.C. Parliament Buildings. From 1906 to 1912, Rattenbury built Vancouver's Neo-Classical Provincial Court House, now home to the Vancouver Art Gallery. The court house was one of many structures that sprung up downtown during the boom years of the early twentieth century. Citizens reveled in "Vancouver's golden years of growth" with a smugness that made the economic crash of 1913 all the more painful. The court house was completed just before the crash, but not the two awkward-looking granodiorite lions—the totem beasts of the British Empire—that rest just outside the building's north entrance. When the money ran out, Scottish sculptor John Bruce halted stonecutting, leaving the beasts manes, noses, and ears unfinished.

The Vancouver Art Gallery, located originally on Georgia Street, was established in 1931. From 1979 to 1982, Arthur Erickson, the city's next most-famous architect after Rattenbury, was given the task of refurbishing the old court house for use by the growing art gallery. Hiring this brilliant—sometimes controversial—architect ensured that the gallery would become a magnet for visitors downtown. Erickson provided for the preservation of the building's turn-of-the-century exterior, while tackling the interior with gusto and style. The elegant new Vancouver Art Gallery opened to grand applause in 1983.

Beyond the gallery's spacious lobby and sinuous spiral staircase are four floors and 41,000 square feet of exhibit space featuring British Columbia's largest collection of artwork. The more than 8,000 pieces range from classical nineteenth-century mountain and landscape paintings to modern conceptual and photo-based works. The gallery's specialty is short-term, traveling exhibits of local and international works. Internationally renowned artists, such as the province's own Jeff Wall, are typical of the groundbreaking collections that have been shown here to great acclaim.

The works of Emily Carr are the unchallenged highlight of the Vancouver Art Gallery. During her life, Carr was overlooked by museums and ignored by the buying public until very late in life. She lived in a ramshackle home on Vancouver Island with her pet dogs and monkey, but made frequent trips to the Queen Charlotte Islands to paint her beloved raincoast forest and the still-magnificent totem poles one sees there today. Finally, in 1937, when she was 65 years old, the Vancouver Art Gallery bought one of her paintings, *Totem Poles, Kitseulka*. (Carr wrote in her diary that she feared the attention might "knock me into conceit"!) That initial purchase would give way to an extensive collection of her works here: 150 paintings and 100 works in other media, 50 of which came from the artist herself before her death in 1945. Some of her most recognizable works, including *Big Raven, Tree Trunk*, and *Scorned as Timber, Beloved of the Sky*, are included in the gallery's impressive collection.

Twentieth-Century Legacies:
Downtown Vancouver &
Beyond

## Christ Church Cathedral

Christ Church Cathedral, located at 690 Burrard Street across from the Fairmont Hotel Vancouver, is the oldest church in the city and one of its oldest stone buildings. It was built between 1889 and 1895 by Winnipeg architect C. O. Wickenden in the Gothic Revival style, which was popular in Canada in the nineteenth century. Like other significant city edifices, the cathedral is made of blocks of cut sandstone from nearby quarries. The interior features wall buttresses, a steep-gabled roof with pointed-arch windows, and Douglas fir ceiling beams that were logged from the old-growth forests that surrounded the young city. Thirty-two stained-glass windows draw on Old and New Testament stories, scenes from Vancouver life, and local plants and animals.

Christ Church was intended to serve the growing population of the city's West End, but money was scarce. Services had been held in the basement— the only room that was finished—since 1889, but in 1891 it was threatened with demolition because it was still unfinished and, frankly, quite unattractive. The church's second rector, Rev. Louis Norman Tucker, promptly enlisted 32-year-old law student J. W. Weart to raise funds. With his help, the church was able to secure a mortgage loan of $18,000. A dedication service was held in the completed building on February 17, 1895. Since that time, the church has been widened, lengthened, and even deepened. In 1978, the building was named a Class A Heritage Site by the municipality of Vancouver and the Province of British Columbia.

In the early years, when the church stood alone on the hill above the harbor, it served as a guiding light to sailors in their vessels below. Since 1929, the church has served as a cathedral and the seat of the New Westminster Anglican Diocese. It is also the regimental church of the Seaforth Highlanders, with 16 memorial plaques and tablets on the walls commemorating their regiments and battalions from the two world wars. When they visit Vancouver, the Royal Family chooses to worship at Christ Church.

# Waterfront Station

Railways have played a major role in British Columbia history since May 23, 1887, when the Canadian Pacific Railway's first transcontinental passenger train arrived on the corner of Cordova and Howe Streets, where Waterfront Station now stands. It was the promise of a railway that convinced British Columbians to join the Dominion of Canada in 1871. When work on the main line from Montreal to the Pacific Coast was completed after seven years, Canadian Pacific Ltd. became one of the most influential companies in Canada. Early residents of Vancouver are said to have remarked, "The government? The CPR's the government here!"

The current Waterfront Station was built in 1914. With its soaring exterior columns and expansive waiting room, it was accurately described by architectural historian Harold Kalman as "self-consciously pompous." The upper walls inside the station are painted with well-known Canadian landscapes, such as the rugged Rocky Mountains and the golden wheatfields of the prairies. Historic markers can be found inside and out, including a plaque marking the arrival of the first passenger train.

To long-time Vancouverites, Waterfront Station remains "the old CPR building." It has become one of the most important hubs of city transportation, providing access to the West Coast Express commuter train as well as SkyTrain, SeaBus, and Translink public transit buses.

## Fairmont Hotel Vancouver

Fairmont Hotel Vancouver is the third in a long and glorious line of château-style hotels built in Vancouver by the Canadian Pacific Railway. All of them were masterfully designed, lavishly appointed, and very popular with the world's wealthy elite of their day. They were also the harbinger of a new era, effectively shifting the city center from the waterfront in today's Gastown to where downtown is today. In May 1888, the first Hotel Vancouver went up in a wasteland of rocks and stumps, but it soon became the new heart of twentieth-century Vancouver.

The second Hotel Vancouver opened on the same site in 1916. Just twelve years later, construction began on the third hotel two blocks west, at the corner of Georgia and Burrard. The Great Depression delayed the project for more than a decade, but when it was announced that King George VI was on his way to Vancouver, it was hurried along again and completed for the historic visit in 1939.

The hotel was designed with French Renaissance details, such as a steep green copper roof, ornate windows, and menacing gargoyles. The exterior is finished with local stone quarried on Haddington Island and displays many elaborate carvings, among them West Coast and Central Plains chiefs, oriental dragons and tigers, and images from Greek mythology, such as winged goats, griffins, and flying horses. Twenty-five varieties of imported marble, totalling 168 tons, decorate the interior.

# Marine Building

When the Marine Building opened at 355 Burrard Street on October 8, 1930, *The Vancouver Sun* rhapsodized, "The building suggests some great marine rock rising from the sea, clinging with sea flora and fauna, tinted in sea green, flashed with gold, at night a dim silhouette piercing the sea mists." Architects John McCarter and George Nairne wanted the design to reflect the various businesses housed within its walls: firms engaged in shipping, lumber, mining, insurance, and import and export trades.

The ambitious project was begun seven months before the onset of the Great Depression, and it nearly bankrupted its owner, Lt.-Cmdr. J. W. Hobbs. Building costs rose from an estimated $1.5 million to $2.3 million. Hobbs managed to finish it—only to be forced to sell it four years later for a paltry $900,000. The new owner, international financier A. J. T. Taylor, left the bottom 21 floors of offices alone, but transformed the penthouse from an observation tower into his personal living quarters.

The Art Deco masterpiece was once the tallest building in the British Empire. Built on a bluff overlooking the harbor, its decor echoes aquatic themes inside and out. The bronze door is carved with crabs, seahorses, and other sea life. Above the front arch are eight historic ships etched in blue-green terra cotta. The north and south sides feature historic ships, including the *Golden Hind* of Sir Francis Drake and the second *Empress of Japan*. The two-story-high lobby, deservedly called the "grand concourse," was designed by John Greed with terra cotta friezes depicting the history of transportation and the colonial discovery of the Pacific Coast. Stained-glass windows depict sunrise and sunset, and fourteen wall sconces are shaped like ships' prows. Classic Art Deco symbols, such as geometric zig-zags, lighting bolts, and sun rays, complete the ornate decor.

117

# Vancouver Lookout! at Harbour Centre

At 581 feet, the Harbour Centre tower on West Hastings Street is British Columbia's tallest building. From the top, called the Vancouver Lookout!, visitors enjoy a 360-degree view of the city. The tower opened on August 13, 1977, with Neil Armstrong, the first man on the moon, officiating at the ceremony. Armstrong's footprints, preserved in concrete, can still be seen on the observation deck.

The lookout is reached in less than 50 seconds by way of a glass-fronted elevator that ascends on the outside of the building. Once arrived, visitors enjoy vistas of the Coast Mountains of the North Shore and Vancouver Island; on a clear day, they can even see as far south as snow-capped Mt. Baker in Washington State. The cruise ship terminal two blocks away at Canada Place, the historic buildings of Gastown, and the low-lying buildings of Chinatown are easy to spot. Maps are conveniently located along the circular observation deck to help visitors orient themselves.

Above Vancouver Lookout!, the Top of Vancouver Revolving Restaurant makes a complete circle every 60 minutes.

Harbour Centre is also home to two levels of shops and services, a 28-floor office tower, and the downtown campus of Simon Fraser

University. The university is another place to get a great view: a small gallery at the north end of the campus lobby has a panoramic window that looks out over the North Shore, an ideal location to get a picture-frame view across the waters of Vancouver Harbour.

*Above: Sunset over Vancouver as seen from the lookout.*

# B C Place Stadium Complex

**B**C Place on Pacific Boulevard is one of Vancouver's most distinctive newer landmarks, built in 1983. It is the largest air-supported stadium in North America, and its impressive white roof dominates the entire east end of False Creek. The roof is made of ten acres of a double-layer of Teflon-coated fiberglass fabric that is only 1/30-of-an-inch thick yet stronger than steel. Air is pumped into a four-foot space between the two layers of fabric, while sixteen electric-powered fans keep the air pressure inside the stadium at a higher level than the air outside, thus preventing the roof from collapsing. Stadium officials note that if the fans were turned off and the doors shut, it would take four to six hours to deflate the roof.

The stadium's sole sports tenant is the B.C. Lions football club, but music concerts, trade shows, and exhibitions are also held here. On July 2nd, 2003, the stadium's 60,000 seats were filled when Vancouver and Whistler were announced as the hosts for the 2010 XXI Olympic Winter Games. The stadium complex also houses the B.C. Sports Hall of Fame and Museum, where interactive exhibits bring British Columbia's sports history and heroes to life with multi-media and hands-on displays.

*Terry Fox Plaza*

*Exhibits honoring great local athletes at the B.C. Sports Hall of Fame and Museum.*

One of the country's best-loved athletes was Terry Fox of Port Coquitlam, British Columbia. When Terry was 18, he lost his right leg to cancer. During his recovery, he vowed to raise money for cancer research. On April 12, 1980, he dipped his artificial leg in the Atlantic Ocean and began his Marathon of Hope. After running halfway across Canada, Fox was forced to stop when cancer struck again. By now a national hero, he wrote in his diary, "I tried as hard as I could, I said I'd never give up and I didn't." Terry Fox died on June 28, 1981 at 22 years of age. Since then, the annual Terry Fox Run has raised millions of dollars for cancer research. The Province of British Columbia even named a peak in the Rocky Mountains Mt. Terry Fox after the courageous young man.

Many Terry Fox memorials have been built across Canada. Vancouver's stands on the upper esplanade of BC Place on Terry Fox Plaza. Franklin Allen built the steel Roman triumphal arch in 1984, guarded by four fiberglass lions, symbols of strength and heroism. Beneath the arch, stainless steel panels depict Terry Fox in his running clothes, opposite a map of Canada showing his route.

*A Grey Cup American football game at BC Place Stadium in July 1987. Photographed by Gunter Marx.*

# Canada Place

Canada Place overlooks Vancouver Harbour at the foot of Granville Street. The building was constructed as the federal pavilion of the government of Canada for Expo 86, Vancouver's 1986 world exposition. Its designers were inspired by the commanding presence of the white, spherical section roofs of the Sydney Opera House in Australia. In that spirit, Canada Place's Teflon-coated roof mimics five billowing white sails, suggesting a fully rigged ship at sea.

The Canada Place complex stretches three city blocks into Burrard Inlet. Pedestrians stroll along its open-air promenade and enjoy the views of Royal Vancouver Yacht Club, Stanley Park, and the Lions Gate Bridge, all prominent city landmarks. The Canada Place Promenade is also one of the very best places from which to view the city's water traffic: The SeaBus ferry hustles back and forth between the adjacent Waterfront Station and West Vancouver's Lonsdale Quay. Fishing vessels stop in at marine fuel stations. Sea planes fly in and out of the harbor. Small pleasure boats and yachts bob along the horizon. And more than 220 luxury cruise ships en route to Alaska dock both here and at the nearby Ballantyne Pier every year. Between May and October, close to one million passengers depart Vancouver to enjoy the famed Vancouver-Alaska cruise, the third most popular cruise destination in the world.

The Canada Place complex is home to the Vancouver Trade and Convention Centre, the World Trade Centre, and the domed Pan Pacific Hotel. At the "prow" is the 440-seat CN IMAX Theatre, with a film format ten times that of conventional 35-mm film. The theater's steeply pitched amphitheater faces a five-story-high screen with six-channel, 14,000-watt digital wraparound sound. Some shows are true sensual experiences, requiring IMAX 3D glasses. The theater is open daily with four different shows, each approximately 40 minutes long.

Across the way from Canada Place is another luxury hotel and the Vancouver Tourist Information Centre, which is open to walk-in visitors. Also located in this historic harbor district is the Art Deco-style Marine Building, Simon Fraser University's Harbour Centre campus, and the Sinclair Centre, a former post office that was converted into shops and offices.

# Science World

Overlooking False Creek on Quebec Street is the best-known of the Expo 86 world exposition legacy buildings, now home to Science World. The building is officially called the Expo Centre, but has been affectionately dubbed "the golf ball." The design is based on the geodesic dome made famous by U.S. inventor and architect Buckminster Fuller. Its mirrorlike exterior panels reflect sunlight and the waters of the creek during the day. At night, 131 exterior lights illuminate the ball.

Science World opened in the Expo Centre in 1989 with five galleries. Unique hands-on exhibits quickly made the "museum" stand out. Children and adults explore scientific phenomena on their own time and terms—sometimes with hilarious results. Exhibits begin in the dinosaur age and end in the space age. Four new permanent galleries have opened since the dawn of the new millennium: Our World, Kidspace, Eureka!, and BodyWorks. The center also develops its own temporary exhibitions, ranging from historical to humorous. For example, *"China! 7000 Years of Innovation"* and *"Grossology: the (Impolite) Science of the Human Body"* have toured North America, Asia, and Europe.

The Alcan OMNIMAX Theatre, with the largest screen in the world, opened in the dome on May 6, 1989. The center has co-produced a number of its films, such as the Academy Award-nominated *The Living Sea* in 1996 and *Everest* in 1998. The steeply raked, 500-seat theater projects images nine times larger than a conventional movie house. Sound pours out of 28 digital speakers backed by 10 tons of equipment.

# Library Square

Controversy swirled around the Vancouver Public Library's central branch before it opened at 350 West Georgia Street on May 29, 1995. What was a Roman amphitheater—a pink one, at that—doing in downtown Vancouver? The question was soon answered with a visit to the building: the soaring new library was a true replacement for the squat, post-World War II former central branch at Burrard and Robson.

New York's Moshe Safdie & Associates, working in partnership with local firm Downs/Archambault and Partners, had been chosen to design the new central branch after a limited architectural competition. Nicknamed the Colosseum, their design includes a nine-story library, an office tower, and brick-red exterior cement walls that contrast starkly with the six-story-high interior glassed concourse. The concourse's coffee shops and cafés quickly became a city meeting place.

Vancouver's first library was set up as an employee reading room in 1869 by J. A. Raymur, manager of the Vancouver Island Spar, Lumber and Sawmill Hastings Mill. The movement to open a permanent library began in 1886 with the opening of a new reading room on Cordova Street in Gastown, whose books were inherited from the old Hastings Mill. The city's first public library, the Carnegie Library, still stands at the corner of Main and Hastings Streets in the Downtown Eastside. Wealthy American industrialist Andrew Carnegie donated $50,000 to open the library in 1903. The city agreed to match that grant with a $5,000 annual donation for upkeep and book purchases. After World War II, the library's collection of 60,000 books had far outgrown the building. On November 1, 1957, its replacement opened at 750 Burrard Street, now a music store. The Carnegie Library in the Carnegie Community Centre continues to serve local residents, many of whom live in older hotels and subsidized rooms in the area.

Vancouver is a city of readers. More than 6.3 million people visit Greater Vancouver's 22 libraries each year, with access to more than 2.6 million items. Free author readings are offered year-round in many of them. The Vancouver International Writers (and Readers) Festival is an annual event, attracting local, national, and international authors to the city for five days every October. *BC BookWorld*, a lively quarterly tabloid of author and publishing news, has done a thriving business for more than 25 years, promoting British Columbia's wealth of writing talent.

*The Miracle Mile*

Eight runners from five countries challenged the men's mile at the 1954 British Empire and Commonwealth Games in Vancouver on August 7, 1954. Two of the runners in Empire Stadium that day, Englishman Roger Bannister and Australia's John Landy, would go down in history when they crossed the finish line in a one-two position, both in under four minutes. Nearing the finish line, Landy was in the lead when he looked over his left shoulder to see where his rival was positioned—and Bannister sped by.

Bannister, who had been the first man to break the four-minute mile on May 6, 1954, won the gold medal at 3:58.8 seconds; Landy ran it at 3:59.6 and took home the silver.

Thirteen years later, in 1967, Landy's famous glance-over-the-shoulder was reproduced in bronze by sculptor John Harman at Vancouver's Harman Sculpture Foundry. The likenesses of the two middle-distance runners are now forever poised in that fateful moment at the entrance to the Pacific National Exhibition grounds on the corner of Hastings and Cassiar Streets.

# Simon Fraser University

"I wanted an experimental university, where new ideas would flourish and creative people would flock in." This vision of Simon Fraser University's first chancellor, Gordon Shrum, still inspires students and faculty more than 40 years after the unique campus opened atop Burnaby Mountain. The university was named after the intrepid Scottish explorer Simon Fraser, the builder of the first colonial trading posts west of the Rocky Mountains between 1810 and 1818.

The university's design was the result of a competition held in 1963. The winner was Arthur Erickson, whose innovative ideas reflected his admiration for the Athens Acropolis and the hill towns of Italy. Erickson set out to harmonize his design with the mountain landscape by terracing the low-slung horizontal buildings. Within a remarkable 18 months, the new university was built and immediately hailed as a triumph. Simon Fraser University opened before a crowd of 5,000 on September 9, 1965—the height of the hippie era. Nicknames for the aerie-like, 430-acre campus included "the instant university," "Radical U," and "Berkeley on the Hill."

At an elevation of 1,200 feet, students live and study in "splendid isolation" on what is still the only mountain-top campus in North America. A 30-minute drive from downtown Vancouver, Simon Fraser's 360-degree view includes Burrard Inlet, the North Shore mountains, fjords, farmlands, the City of Vancouver, and its suburbs.

The university has two other campuses: one at Harbour Centre in downtown Vancouver, and the award-winning Surrey Campus, designed by internationally renowned Vancouver architect Bing Thom. Total enrollment at SFU is more than 25,000 students.

# Grouse Mountain

To Vancouverites, Grouse Mountain is a watchful friend, presiding at the top of North Vancouver's Capilano Road at 4,500 feet above sea level. The mountain was named by hikers in 1894 for the blue grouse that populate the area. As the closest of the Coast Mountain peaks, Grouse was one of the first to be developed as an outdoor destination: local hikers and skiers have been enjoying the mountain since the 1890s. By 1910, Grouse was so popular that planning began for a railroad to the summit to eliminate the arduous climb to the top. The advent of World War I ended that endeavor, but in 1949 the mountain's first ski lift was installed, noteworthy as the world's first double-chair lift.

Grouse has always attracted year-round visitors. Determined summer hikers challenge the steep and rugged two-mile Grouse Grind trail to the top. The arrival of the first snow is noted with anticipation by skiers and snowboarders, who soon make their way to the runs. Today's visitors can park in a convenient lot at the base of the mountain, then take a spectacular eight-minute ride on the enclosed Grouse Mountain Skyride gondola to the mountain's first level, 3,700 feet above sea level. From here, the Peak Chair completes the ascent to 4,100 feet, where visitors enjoy a 360-degree view that includes Vancouver Island across the Strait of Georgia.

At the 3,700-foot level, the indoor Theatre in the Sky presents *Born to Fly*, an eagle-eye view of British Columbia shot in high-definition video. Nearby, in an alpine forest setting on the shore of Blue Grouse Lake, the *hiwus* Feasthouse and Cultural Centre honors and shares Pacific Northwest Coast Native traditions and cuisine with group bookings. Housed in a cedar long-house raised on massive timbers and decorated with ornate carvings, the *hiwus* experience is guaranteed authentic by members of the Squamish Nation and Sechelt Band, who perform startling mask dances for guests in a fire-lit room.

The Refuge for Endangered Wildlife, one of the mountain's newest attractions, is an enclosed, two-acre outdoor habitat. The refuge is home to three wolves and orphaned grizzly bears Grinder and Coola, both of whom arrived in 2001. The larger bear, Coola, is a Coastal grizzly, which eats salmon as part of its natural diet. Grinder, an Interior grizzly, consumes a diet of up to 85 percent vegetation. In the summertime, peregrine falcons, red-tailed hawks, a golden eagle, and a barred owl join the grizzly pair in the refuge.

*Opposite: Grizzly Bear.*
*Right: Wolf.*

# *University of British Columbia*

Iistory and heritage have distinguished the University of British Columbia (UBC) since it became a degree-granting institution in 1915. Its first students attended classes in warehouses and church basements near Vancouver's City Hall. A plan to move the campus to scenic Point Grey overlooking the Strait of Georgia was sidelined by World War I. After the war, returning students gathered in frustration and walked from downtown Vancouver to Point Grey to make their wishes clear to the government. The "Great Trek" was effective: in 1925, the new campus opened 20 minutes from downtown Vancouver.

Today, UBC is a city unto itself. Every day, more than 45,000 people circulate on the huge campus. Hence, in addition to all the buildings required to teach its more than 35,000 full- and part-time students, the university includes extensive housing developments, concert halls, theaters, gardens, galleries, athletic centers, food courts, and cafés. Campus architecture includes both historic and modern styles. Several of the original buildings still exist, such as the Main Library, whose stained-glass windows, brass fittings, and stone masonry are classic examples of the Neo-Gothic architecture that

*Walter C. Koerner Library*

*Royal Bank Cinema.*

was popular in Vancouver in the 1920s. Other notable buildings include the UBC Museum of Anthropology, the nearby First Nations Longhouse, and the Asian Centre. Students in the Native Indian Teacher Education Program (NITEP) study in the traditional-style longhouse, which is built of cedar and glass and supported by sculpted lodge poles. The Asian Centre's home is a former pavilion from Expo 70 in Osaka, Japan.

To the delight of UBC students, an abundance of parks and gardens dot their campus. The outstanding 1,885-acre forest-and-bog landscape of Pacific Spirit Regional Park draws even non-students to its extensive trail network between Point Grey and the Fraser River. Beaches and high bluffs add to the park's diversity. The 70 acres of rare and unusual plants at the UBC Botanical Garden and Centre for Plant Research are more subdued, but equally enjoyable. Established in 1916, the garden is the oldest continuously operating university botanical park in Canada, with fascinating displays of native, Asian, and alpine plants. UBC's famed Rose Garden overlooking the Pacific bursts with a rainbow of 300 varieties of petaled beauties that bloom almost year-round. Japanese landscape architect Kannosuke Mori designed the Nitobe Memorial Garden, named after Inazo Nitobe, an important Japanese educator and statesman. Many native Japanese trees and shrubs, small ponds, bridges, and a ceremonial Tea House make the site a delightful spot to stroll or picnic.

The university continues to grow every day. The next big project in the pipeline is University Town, an eight-neighborhood housing development that will accommodate 20,000 more students, faculty, staff, and off-campus purchasers when completed.

Coal Harbour

## Royal Vancouver Yacht Club

Vancouver is a boater's delight, surrounded by the waters of the Pacific Ocean, with English Bay, Burrard Inlet, Howe Sound, and the Strait of Georgia all readily accessible from the city. The Royal Vancouver Yacht Club was founded in 1903 to take advantage of this delightful arrangement. Today it has two marinas in Vancouver and six outstations in strategic locations in the Gulf Islands as well as up the West Coast as far as Desolation Sound. The main clubhouse is at Jericho Beach in Point Grey, with docking for most of the sailboats of its 5,000 members. The second marina, at Coal Harbour in Stanley Park, is home to powerboats and some sailboats.

The City of Vancouver's apt motto is "By Sea, Land and Air We Prosper." Indeed, it was the prosperous businessmen at the turn of the century who founded the yacht club. Having their own club was a point of honor for the town's boaters, the city's up-and-coming movers and shakers. These days the club's membership is more diverse, as Commodore A. J. Patrick Oswald noted: "We are a multifaceted club. Our membership ranges from world-class sailors to family cruising members. Our interests vary from one-design racing to offshore cruising. Our pride in the Royal Vancouver Yacht Club unites us all."

*Jericho Beach*

# Capilano Suspension Bridge

George Grant Mackay, an intrepid Scottish outdoorsman, was elected park commissioner of Vancouver soon after he moved here in 1888. The energetic 62-year-old bought 6,000 acres of old-growth rainforest along the Capilano River in what is now North Vancouver and built a cabin on the edge of the canyon wall. He had just one problem in his new home: he couldn't get to the portion of his property on the other side of the river. So, with the help of two Coast Salish men and a team of horses, he built a small suspension bridge using hemp rope and cedar planks. His helpers called it the "laughing bridge" because of the noise it made when the wind blew. News of the bridge traveled fast, and it immediately became a curiosity. People from all over hiked to Mackay's property to try it out—so many, in fact, that they were nicknamed "Capilano Tramps."

In 1903, ten years after Mackay's death, the

hemp and cedar bridge was replaced by a wire cable bridge. The 450-foot crossing is still as challenging as it was in MacKay's days and, even though it is now strong enough to support 10 military fighter planes, looking down 230 feet to the Capilano River is an unforgettable thrill. As the world's longest and highest suspension footbridge, the Capilano now attracts 750,000 visitors a year, and is recognized by Attractions Canada and the National Tourism Excellence Award as British Columbia's best and most innovative outdoor attraction.

After crossing the bridge, visitors find plenty more to do in the park surrounding the Capilano Suspension Bridge. The park is kept in a constant state of self-improvement—the better to fascinate its guests. Currently, replanting and reseeding projects are going on, and recently the park's owners added Treetops Adventure. On this walk through the treetops of the 300-year-old rainforest, visitors cross between Douglas firs on elevated suspension bridges, some as high as 100 feet above the forest floor. To protect the delicate environment, an innovative compression system secures each tree's observation platform using only 20 pounds of force per square inch: about the amount of pressure exerted by pressing a thumb firmly on a tabletop. A system of raised boardwalks also allows visitors to walk along the forest floor without harming it. Among the park's other interesting features are Totem Park, a display of locally carved poles collected since the 1930s; the Big House, where visitors are invited to watch and talk with First Nations carvers at work; the Story Centre, which tells the history of the park and of North Vancouver; and an English country garden that features azaleas and rhododendrons.

*Horseshoe Bay*

Horseshoe Bay is a hilly West Vancouver hamlet on Howe Sound with about 1,000 residents. The bay's original Coast Salish name was *Chai-hai*, which refers to a low sizzling noise. Some believe this was the noise made by the fish that were once plentiful here. Captain George Vancouver named Howe Sound, an ocean fjord, after Admiral Richard Scrope, Earl Howe, who defeated the French fleet in 1794. The sound stretches 25 miles from Horseshoe Bay to Squamish. The oldest rocks in the Vancouver area are found just north of Horseshoe Bay. At least 185 million years old, they combine sedimentary and volcanic components that were once buried deep underground.

To escape the pollution of industrial Vancouver at the turn of the nineteenth century, wealthy families would travel by train or steamer to Horseshoe Bay during the hot summer months. The bay's sheltered beach was ideal for bathing and picnicking. Some of the city's wealthy citizens even built summer homes here. Gustav Roedde, for example, Vancouver's first bookbinder, built a cottage here by shipping it in sections from Vancouver. Every summer, the bookbinder brought his employees out on the railway for their annual picnic.

The pioneering Sewell family moved into Roedde's cottage on Horseshoe Bay in 1931. Dan Sewell made his living as a boat builder and by running the marina, which still exists today. In 1995, Tom Sewell, Dan's son, recalled his childhood in the 1930s: "Horseshoe Bay was just a collection of cottages, a favorite weekend spot for campers, picnickers and fishers. Sunday outings to the neighboring islands were especially popular. In winter, the bay rolled up its sidewalks. Just a few pioneer families lived here year-round. Those were lean years. We started business in a primitive way. We knew how to drive nails so between us we built our first floats and boats."

Today, Horseshoe Bay is best known as the British Columbia Ferries terminal for passengers and cars en route to Vancouver Island. An inviting park curves along the bay with a playground, benches, and a long wooden dock; just steps away are restaurants and shops. The two totem poles displayed in the park are the work of coastal carvers: The Kwakiutl bear pole was carved in 1966 by Tony Hunt of the Kwawkewlth Band of Victoria. The second pole was carved in 1975 by Tsimshian chief William Jeffrey and his son Rupert.

# The Great Outdoors:
# Whistler

*Previous page: Whistler Mountain across Alta Lake.*

## Shannon Falls Provincial Park

Hidden in a West Coast rainforest just before Squamish on the way from Vancouver, Shannon Falls is one of dozens of permanent and semi-permanent glacier-fed waterfalls along Highway 99. At 1,105 feet, it is the third-highest waterfall in British Columbia. Shannon Falls Provincial Park, established in 1984, is visited by more than half a million people every year.

Visitors walking the short distance through the rainforest to the falls soon hear the roaring of glacial waters tumbling over a granite precipice into a crystal-clear creek below. A short climb farther leads to a viewing platform, so close to the falls that water sprays visitors with a fine mist. In May, the waters are at their peak, heavy with spring runoff from the Coast Mountains. The air is cool and refreshing all summer long; in winter, if the temperature is low enough, ice climbers tackle the frozen falls.

Scientists say Shannon Falls was formed more than 13,000 years ago during a period of glaciation, when glacial ice reached the height of the top of the falls. A Coast Salish legend offers another view of their origin: A great serpent, Say'noth'kai, left his home in Howe Sound to explore the mountains. His repeated slithering journeys wore down the rock here, thus creating Shannon Falls.

# Stawamus Chief

Rising 2,064 feet above the town of Squamish, the Stawamus Chief is the second-largest granite monolith in the world. To the Coast Salish people who are now known as the Squamish Nation, the great rock resembles a chief asleep on his side. More than 100,000 years ago, the glacial ice that covered this area retreated and the Squamish Valley deepened. The hardest rocks withstood the grinding onslaught and were polished smooth. No finer example of this exists than the Stawamus Chief, created by the sandpaper-like friction of rock against moving ice.

More than 50,000 people hike or climb the Chief's three peaks every year. Three strenuous trail hikes run up the backside of the wall, but many rock climbers tackle the challenge by going straight up the Grand Wall at the Highway 99 parking lot. In 1997, British Columbia designated the Chief and his surrounding 1,250 acres as the Stawamus Chief Provincial Park. Climbers were not the only ones to benefit from the designation: since the mid-1980s, the southwest face of the Chief has been home to endangered Peregrine falcons. Climbers are happy to avoid certain mid-elevation routes between March 15 and July 31, when the Peregrines raise their young.

*Stawamus* is a more accurate Coast Salish spelling of *Squamish*, which means "mother of the wind." The area is so named for the powerful north winds that are tunneled from the interior of British Columbia along the Cheakamus and Squamish Valleys. They can be fierce, with winter gusts averaging 40 knots an hour and rising as high as 70 knots. Windsurfing at the mouth of the Squamish River is among the best in North America.

*Stawamus Chief is the finest example of rock shaped by the friction against moving ice.*

*The West Coast Railway Heritage Park*

# Squamish

The town of Squamish began life as an agricultural community in the late 1800s. By 1902, logging had overtaken farming as the area's main industry, and it still plays an important role in the economy of the Squamish Valley today. Squamish Logger Days, a sports event held annually during the August 1 long weekend, celebrates the area's colorful and rugged past.

The logging town is now home to more than 15,000 permanent residents, many of whom commute daily to Whistler or Vancouver. The Squamish First Nations people who are native to the area still comprise an active community here, involved in cultural activities, traditional education, and environmental preservation. When Captain George Vancouver anchored in Howe Sound in 1792, he was close to their ancestors' 16 villages along the Squamish River, but he didn't know it at the time.

Nowadays, Squamish is known as the "Gateway to Recreation." In addition to the Stawamus Chief, a rock climbers' paradise, the town provides access to many lakes and parks, including Lake Lovely Water Recreational Area, Alice Lake Provincial Park, and Diamond Head

in Garibaldi Provincial Park. Mountain biking, rock climbing, hiking, windsufing, and boating are popular activities here.

Another area attraction is a natural phenomenon of great power and beauty. Every winter, the annual salmon runs in the Squamish River draw as many as 2,000 bald eagles to its banks, inspiring an annual eagle-watching festival in Brackendale, a village five minutes north of Squamish. The white-headed birds of prey roost in the cottonwood trees that line the river. Although they can be seen throughout the area, they are best viewed from the Eagle Watch Interpretive Centre on Government Road. Bald eagles are respected by First Nations people for their power and spirituality; to see an eagle is considered to be a blessing and a sign of protection.

The area's railroad heritage is significantly displayed at the West Coast Railway Heritage Park, Western Canada's largest collection of heritage railway equipment. Among the more than 70 vintage railway cars and locomotives dating back to 1890 is the famed Royal Hudson Steam Train #2860, whose throaty whistle has been described as "the sound of summer."

# Whistler Village Gondola

The first Whistler Mountain gondola lifted off at Creekside in 1965. One of the four-seater originals now sits outside the Whistler Museum and Archives in Village North, reminding visitors how far ski technology has come in the past 40 years. Eventually, the gondola linked skiers to a t-bar lift that moved them into high alpine powder, opening up the peak and back bowl.

Today, the Whistler Village Gondola is Whistler Blackcomb's fastest lift. It leaves Whistler Village traveling 1,100 feet per minute; in just under 20 minutes, it rises 6,000 feet to the Roundhouse Lodge. Whistler's local newspaper, *The Pique*, named the gondola its top pick in the category of best places to make out. The 360-degree view offers a vista of the resort, Whistler valley, lakes, slopes, and the jagged peaks of Black Tusk to the south. Luckily for lovers, the gondola runs both winter and summer.

In winter, the gondola is one of 20 lifts that take skiers and snow-boarders up the mountain to access more than 100 runs. Lift capacity is 30,000 people every hour. From the enclosed gondola, five giant bowls can be seen above the treeline: Symphony Bowl, Harmony Bowl, Glacier Bowl, Whistler Bowl, and West Bowl, all of which are served by two high-speed quads, Harmony Express and the Peak. In summer, sightseers join the hundreds of mountain bikers who ride the Whistler Village Gondola every day. While the former mosy along exploring the mountain's 30 miles of hiking trails and turquoise alpine lakes, the latter hurtle through the meadows down the 3,937-foot descent in a blur of greens, blues, reds, and yellows. Marmots, the large whistling squirrels for whom Whistler was named, amuse visitors by playing hide and seek in piles of rocks along the lakes.

# Whistler Mountain

Whistler Mountain is part of the Fitzsimmons Range of the Coast Mountains, with a formidable backrop of seven volcanic peaks to the north. Coast Salish and Interior Salish people have crossed these mountains for thousands of years. Small enclaves of Europeans began popping up here during the Fraser Gold Rush of the late 1850s. From 1914 to 1948, Alex and Myrtle Philip ran their popular Rainbow Lodge on Alta Lake, effectively putting Whistler on the map. By the 1950s, Whistler Mountain's reputation for its perfect powder snows and panoramic views of Whistler Valley was widespread. With a top elevation of 7,160 feet and an average annual snowfall of more than 30 feet on the summits, the mountain became known as a skier's paradise.

But without a road in, only a dedicated few were lucky enough to experience this paradise. One of the mountain's most devoted skiers, Norwegian Franz Wilhelmsen, joined with a group of businessmen to try to solve that problem. Their first scheme to develop the area—by attracting the Winter Olympic Games to Whistler—was unsuccessful. They tried again by forming the Garibaldi Lift Company, which officially opened the mountain's first gondola and chair lift system in 1966. Once people no longer had to climb up the mountain to ski down, Whistler quickly turned into a booming resort area.

Today, the "godfather of Whistler skiing" has his own run: the five-mile Franz's Run, one of the longest in North America. In 2003, Whistler and Vancouver were awarded the 2010 Olympic and Paralympic Winter Games—finally fulfilling Wilhelmsen's greatest hope for the mountain.

# Blackcomb Mountain

**B**lackcomb Mountain is located in the Spearhead Range of the Coast Mountains. Area pioneer and resort operator Alex Philip, an animated storyteller who often entertained visitors with his knowledge of the local mountains, is said to have had a hand in naming this majestic, "mile-high" mountain: he described the serrated peak of what is now Blackcomb Mountain as a rooster's comb, only black instead of red.

A sister to Whistler Mountain, Blackcomb opened for business on December 6, 1980, fifteen years after Whistler Mountain's first gondola lifted skiers to the high alpine. A healthy rivalry developed between them, resulting in bigger and better facilities for both. In 1986, Joe Houssian, president of Intrawest Corporation, bought Blackcomb Mountain from its original owners. A decade later, Blackcomb and Whistler merged operations under the Intrawest banner. Intrawest is now the biggest ski resort developer in North America, and the two mountains have become the continent's largest skiing, snowboarding, and resort experience. So far, the company has developed two hotel and shopping zones at the bases of the mountains: Upper Village at the base of Blackcomb Mountain and Village North between the two mountains.

Like Whistler Mountain, Blackcomb is open winter and summer. In the winter, 17 lifts carry more than 29,000 passengers per hour from three bases: Upper Village Blackcomb Base, Excalibur Village Station, and Excalibur Base II. The mountain's enormous terrain of 3,314 acres provides for spectacular skiing and snowboarding. More than 100 runs include double black diamond turns in the high alpine, green runs below for novices, and every level of difficulty in between. The longest ski run on the mountain is 7 miles. Summer activities include mountain biking, scenic viewing, and skiing and snowboarding on Blackcomb's two glaciers.

# Rainbow Park

Rainbow Park, at the north end of Alta Lake, marks the original settlement of Rainbow, a whistle-stop on the B.C. Rail line. It recalls the old days in Whistler, when summer was the preferred season for recreation and winter in the mountains was avoided. The seed for Whistler's astonishing growth into a year-round international resort was planted in 1908. That year, in a restaurant in downtown Vancouver, a young waiter named Alex Philip met John Millar, a grizzled, Texas-born cowboy-turned-trapper. Millar's stories of a pristine wilderness further north appealed to Alex's romantic nature. Ultimately, they inspired him and his young wife, Myrtle, to leave the comforts of the city for the wilds of the Coast Mountains.

The Philips made their home in Whistler Valley and, with the help of Myrtle's industrious father, opened Rainbow Lodge on Alta Lake in 1914. It was soon the most popular resort west of the Rockies, drawing avid crowds of summer visitors to hike, fish for trout, climb mountains, canoe, sail, and ride horses. The active couple retired in 1948, having contributed much to the community. Alex passed away in 1968; Myrtle died in 1986; and the historic lodge burned down in 1977.

Nevertheless, happy reminders of the bygone era of Rainbow Lodge can still be seen at Rainbow Park. The cabin of Sewell Tapley, Myrtle's father, is still here, as is a replica of Alex Philip's famous Bridge of Sighs. Today, the park has a beach, picnic and barbecue facilities, a dock, volleyball courts, and excellent views of Whistler and Blackcomb Mountains. Rainbow Mountain, Rainbow Falls, Rainbow Lake, Rainbow Canyon, and Rainbow Creek are also located in the area.

*View of Alta Lake from Rainbow Park.*

# Golf at Whistler

Golf began along the Sea to Sky corridor with Horseshoe Bay's Gleneagles Course in June 1927. Scottish architect A. V. Macan's design has the first hole at Gleneagles played 296 yards straight up a hill—the hole was appropriately named "Cardiac Hill." These days, golfers can choose from six courses between Horseshoe Bay and Pemberton. Four of the most spectacular are in Whistler, which takes advantage of its mountain setting to design exceptionally challenging courses with breathtaking views.

Whistler's "Big Four" golf courses are all 18-hole, par-72 courses on over 6,000 acres each, and they all boast lush greens, luxury amenities, and competitive service. The first on the scene was the Whistler Golf Club, opened in 1983. The club was the first Canadian design by golf legend Arnold Palmer. Its nine lakes, two picturesque creeks, rolling greens, and mountain vistas set the tone for future courses in the area: the Fairmont Château Whistler Golf Club, designed by another golf great, Robert Trent Jones Jr.; Bob Cupp's Big Sky Golf & Country Club in Pemberton at the base of the 8,000-foot Mount Currie; and Whistler's Nicklaus North Golf Course, which opened with golfer and designer Jack Nicklaus playing an exhibition round—his first in British Columbia in 30 years.

Whistler never planned to be a golf destination. The sport came as a sidebar to the area's growth as an all-season resort. Now that it has arrived, though, investors have made the most of its presence. All of the Big Four courses have earned four stars from *Golf Digest*, and Whistler is rated one of the top golf destinations in Canada today.

*The Fairmont Château Whistler Golf Club's #8 hole.*

153

# Mt. Tantalus

Vancouver's Coast Mountain range is often confused with the Rocky Mountains because both run along the borders of British Columbia. The Coast Mountains run along the west coast of the Pacific Ocean for 1,056 miles to the Yukon and east to the interior plateaus. The Rockies define the eastern border between the provinces of British Columbia and Alberta.

The Coast Mountains were formed by a gradual uplifting from the cool underground 100 million years ago. Several ice ages followed, the last of which was 13,000 years ago, when a 5,000-foot-thick glacier covered this area as far south as present-day Seattle. The Coast Mountains continue to rise several fractions of an inch every century, but erode by a similar amount.

Two peaks, Mt. Tantalus and Mt. Garibaldi, stand out in the ranges south of Whistler. At 8,540 feet, Mt. Tantalus is the highest peak in the Tantalus Mountain Range, a series of impressive peaks that rises above the Squamish Valley along the Pacific Ocean. Several other peaks in the range are notable: Mt. Niobe, at 6,600 feet, is the highest mountain at the southwest end of Lake Lovely Water. Mt. Serratus, at 7,600 feet, is famous for its glaciers.

Mt. Garibaldi is an 8,787-foot mountain in the Pacific Ring of Fire, a great arc of volcanic activity. In 1860, the mountain was named after Guiseppe Garibaldi, a nineteenth-century Italian hero and patriot. The 480,000-acre Garibaldi Provincial Park, created in 1920 to take advantage of the area's popularity, remains the most popular of British Columbia's provincial parks. Volcanic action formed many of the peaks here, each unique in appearance. Their names tell their stories: the Table, Cinder Cone, Glacier Pikes, Black Tusk.

*Alex Philip's Bridge of Sighs crosses the river he romantically named the River of Golden Dreams.*

## River of Golden Dreams

In 1914, resort pioneers Myrtle and Alex Philip built the first fishing lodge on Alta Lake. Today, Rainbow Lodge is gone, but a memorial site in Rainbow Park features a replica of Alex Philip's Bridge of Sighs. The bridge crosses a stream that is officially named Alta Creek, but is marked on all maps as the River of Golden Dreams—the name given to it by the people's favorite romantic, Alex.

"Newlyweds would come up and Alex wanted a place for them to hold hands and gaze into each other's eyes and sigh. The bridge was such a place," explained Whistler historian Florence Petersen. Before Myrtle's death in 1986, Petersen spent many hours interviewing her about the early history of the area. She told of how her husband used to paddle newlyweds across Alta Lake on moonlit nights, canoeing along the River of Golden Dreams, crossing Lilypad Flat, and heading up the river to Green Lake.

The route along the River of Golden Dreams twists and turns through wetlands where beavers make their dams, mink glide through the waters, and many species of birds and waterfowl nest in the reeds along the shore. Near Green Lake, the peaks of Mount Currie and Blackcomb and Wedge Mountains tower overhead. Visitors still canoe and kayak along the crystal clear river, just as Alex loved to do in the early days of Rainbow Lodge.

# Whistler Interpretive Forest

Within the 7,412 acres of the Whistler Interpretive Forest, visitors discover a wide variety of landscapes, trees, geological formations, and fish and wildlife habitats just minutes from Whistler Village. The unique, free forest is a living classroom, with elevation rising from 1,968 feet to more than 5,249 feet. Large, panelled information signs, interpretive sites, forestry demonstrations, and other educational features are located inside the working forest area. Six easy-to-moderate hikes and a driving tour cover 9 miles of trails, with stops of interest marked along the way.

Over the centuries, natural phenomena, logging, and, more recently, a rise in nearby recreational activity have altered the forest's landscape. In order to preserve its natural, native beauty, Whistler foresters have combined the remnants of original old-growth stands with a variety of tree plantations that were introduced after clear-cutting. Two bio-geoclimatic zones are found in the area: coastal Western hemlock zone, which covers most of the forest, and mountain hemlock zone at higher elevations. Every autumn, Whistler's forests come alive with colors. Dark green conifers are a backdrop for the bright yellows of cottonwood and birch, and the varied oranges and reds of alder. The yellow leaves of the devil's club resemble those of the big leaf maple, but are armed with prickly spines.

# Whistler Villages

In the 1960s, Whistler struggled as a ski resort, hampered by the area's isolation and inaccessibility. The area's reputation as a back-country ski spot was only reinforced by its ramshackle buildings and cast of famously eccentric characters. By 1977, it was obvious that Whistler could not continue to grow without a long-term vision and focused development.

On an exploratory visit to the established ski resort of Vail, Colorado, Whistler alderman Garry Watson and Al Raine, the province's first coordinator of ski development, met designer Eldon

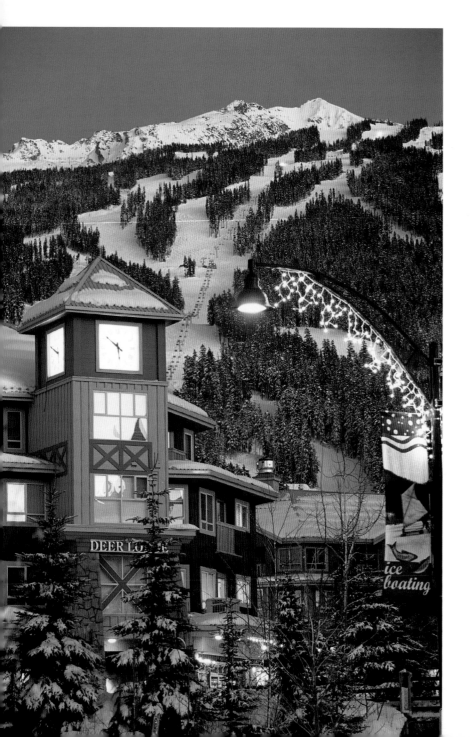

Beck, an American landscape architect based in San Francisco. They liked Beck's style, and so soon had him working on the plans for Whistler Village, a pedestrian-only, alpine-style design that Beck created from European models. The chosen site, at the foot of both Whistler and Blackcomb Mountains, was 58 acres in size—some of which had been the local garbage dump. When Whistler Village opened in 1980 around Village Square, visitors found they could ski from their hotel rooms to the lifts. The concept was an immediate success, winning many design awards.

Soon, other villages followed. Upper Village, at the foot of Blackcomb Mountain, is just a short walk across Fitzsimmons Creek from Whistler Village. The 24-hectare Village North, with its $25 million Whistler Town Square and Marketplace, grew out of an unpaved, pothole-marked parking lot. And Whistler Creekside, actually the original village in the resort area, has been transformed from a quiet backwater that was too far from "the action" to attract guests into lively competition for its three sister villages.

Now, more than two million people visit Whistler every year. Visitors can choose from more than 115 hotels, 90 restaurants and bars,

200 shops and services, and three golf courses, with a fourth nearby. In addition, the four villages offer tour companies, a movie house, a conference center, grocery stores, a shopping mall, post offices, a multi-faceted arts center, and a cultural center featuring First Nations performers and artists—not to mention a plethora of ski lifts and gondolas. Since 1991, the resort's popularity has repeatedly earned it the title of top ski resort in North America. Whistler's reputation will only continue to grow: on July 2, 2003, the International Olympic Committee chose Vancouver-Whistler to host the 2010 Olympic and Paralympic Winter Games.